The Thinking Books

The Thinking Books

Susan Swan
and
Richard White

The Falmer Press
(A member of the Taylor & Francis Group)
London • Washington, D.C.

UK The Falmer Press, 4 John Street, London WC1N 2ET
USA The Falmer Press, Taylor & Francis Inc., 1900 Frost Road, Suite 101, Bristol, PA 19007

First published in 1994

A catalogue record for this book is available from the British Library

Library of Congress Cataloging-in-Publication Data are available on request

ISBN 0 7507 0295 8 (paper)

Jacket design by Claude Sironi

Typeset in 12/14 pt Bembo by
Graphicraft Typesetters Ltd., Hong Kong.

Printed in Great Britain by Burgess Science Press, Basingstoke on paper which has a specified pH value on final paper manufacture of not less than 7.5 and is therefore 'acid free'.

Contents

Preface vii
1 Early Days 1
2 Krysia 15
3 Learning Together 24
4 Ariana 29
5 Learning to Question 37
6 Anna 49
7 Arthur 59
8 Revelations of Understanding 70
9 Stephanie 79
10 Jenny's Book 88
11 Myself as a Reflective Teacher 112
12 Five Years Later 117
Index 126

Preface

This is a story of change. It tells how one of us, Susan, set about changing how the 8-year-old children in her third grade class learned, and how in doing so she changed herself. Her experiences with the thinking books also changed how both of us think about teaching and learning, and about what it is possible to achieve in primary school.

The story shows how these young children learned what it means to learn, and how they became more purposeful, reflective and questioning in class. It tells how individuals changed, for instance how Stephanie was saved from wasted years of unproductive passive dependence, how Ariana grew in confidence, how Arthur learned purpose without losing his taste for creative fantasy.

Our book has two authors, but we wrote it in the first person singular, with Susan as the narrator, to maintain the directness of our account of what happened when grade 3S worked with their thinking books.

Chapter One

Early Days

I watched the children leave. Eight-year-olds have a lot of energy still at the end of the school day, at least more than their teacher usually has.

'Bye, Vicky, bye, Tim, bye, Paul, see you tomorrow.'

'Bye, Mrs Swan. Don't forget our thinking books.'

No chance of that. The thinking books were stacked on my table, for me to read and write in before I left. Catherine's was on top.

Catherine: 24 March

Today
I Lent that a Dictiory dasnt
have evry sigl werd in it.
And Whot's the uos of a
Dictiory that hasnt ben
finst. You have to be cefl
with a Dictiory lillk this.
walle if you by a book for

29$ just for one werd and
it wosnt in the book it wood of ben
a wast of money thats mony donw
the dran.

Catherine's spelling is poor, I know, and I would have to do something about it, but I did not correct it in her thinking book. I would work on it another time. What pleased me was the evidence that this not especially bright 8-year-old with poor language skills had thought about what she had learned that day, had come up with a personal opinion, and had expressed it vigorously and clearly. Besides, I liked the drawing of the money going down the drain.

Catherine is one of twenty-one children in my grade 3. We work at Clayton North Primary School, in a suburb of Melbourne. We are all Australian, but about half of the children were born in other countries. Only six have parents born in Australia, others come from Greece, Italy, Turkey, Egypt, Fiji, Cook Islands, the United States, Sri Lanka, Poland and Yugoslavia. Three spoke no English at the beginning of the year. There are only five boys. One girl is intellectually disabled. We are a mixed lot.

On the first day of the school year I looked at the children and they looked at me. This was a big day for them. They had now moved up from the infants' section to the middle school. I always enjoy the beginning of a new school year – the same feeling of promise and great intentions that I have when I am about to write in a new exercise book, all those beautiful blank pages just waiting to be filled. Of course, as the year goes on it is harder to be so positive. Every year on this first day the daily newspapers run a photograph of some small child starting school, but that seems to be the last sympathetic report schools will get. You do not have to wait long for expressions of concern from educators, parents, employers and the general public that education is not meeting the needs of today's society. And unfortunately it is true that students often learn passively, copying notes and learning by rote, with no idea of the purpose of lessons.

I knew of Ross Tasker's interviews with high school students during science lessons:

> [Pupil] 'He talked about it . . . That's about all . . .'
> [Interviewer] 'What have you decided it (the task) is about?'
> [Pupil] 'I dunno, I never really thought about it . . . just doing it – doing what it says . . . its 8.5 . . . just got to do different numbers and the next one we have to do is this (points in text to 8.6).'
>
> . . . . .
>
> [Interviewer] (joining a group of three boys) 'This looks interesting.'
> [Pupil] 'Yeah, we have to . . . fill the beaker to 150 . . . then um . . . get 5ml of salt, then we put it in here (indicating the beaker of water) and then we put it on there (touching the gauze on the tripod) – then we have to take the heat.'
> [Interviewer] 'I see and what's it all about?'
> [Pupil] 'I dunno – we just have to do it and get the graph.'
>
> (Tasker, 1981, p. 34)

And of the time when Damien Hynes wrote nonsense notes in a year 10 geography class, and, as one of his students wrote later:

> In mid-term 1, we were asked to copy two paragraphs of notes from the board so, being students we did. (Dibley, 1986, p. 88)

I have often thought about that admission, 'being students we did'. The student went on:

> We didn't think about what we were writing . . . we were instructed to ask questions about anything we didn't understand. A few of us did this, but not many . . . Maybe we all understood, or believed we did. At least we were all ready to leave the classroom then and there with our notes as they were, so imagine our embarrassment when we found the notes were meaningless, made up by Mr Hynes. (*ibid*)

I also knew about studies that showed that students in high school and at university who were successful in passing examinations often lacked real understanding. I had read, for instance, about engineering students who could not put together a dry cell, wire and globe in a way that made the globe light, university physics students who thought that there is almost no gravity at the top of Mt Everest, and medical students who thought that grandchildren of whites who went to live in the tropics would become black.

When I thought back to my own time in school, these results rang true. A few days before I had looked over a high school test I had done on biology, and found I could recall hardly anything of even the basic concepts. My own learning had been shallow and without true understanding.

I also knew from my own teaching that children often construct remarkable meanings for what they are told, meanings that indicate that they probably have not thought deeply about the information. One example of this occurred very early in my career when I was a student teacher in my final year. I was teaching a third grade and had been requested by my supervising teacher to teach 'the water cycle' which was part of the prescribed science course for the third grade.

I prepared a very standard lesson using one of the most common models of the water cycle: a kettle was boiled and a chilled plate held over the top of the spout. As expected the water vapour condensed on the plate, drops of water ran down the plate and fell on the desk.

The lesson appeared very successful. The children were all very interested and participated in the lesson discussion with some enthusiasm. Many of the children were quite excited; they could relate this to things in their everyday lives. They could see why water drops ran down the window when dinner was cooking and why the bathroom mirror fogged up when they had a bath. I was feeling quite satisfied with the lesson and confident that the children had understood the water cycle.

I then asked the children to each create a drawing to explain the water cycle and to write down any questions which they had about it.

The various problems the children had with understanding the water cycle then emerged. The demonstration model I had used in my lesson had led to some difficulties in the children's understanding.

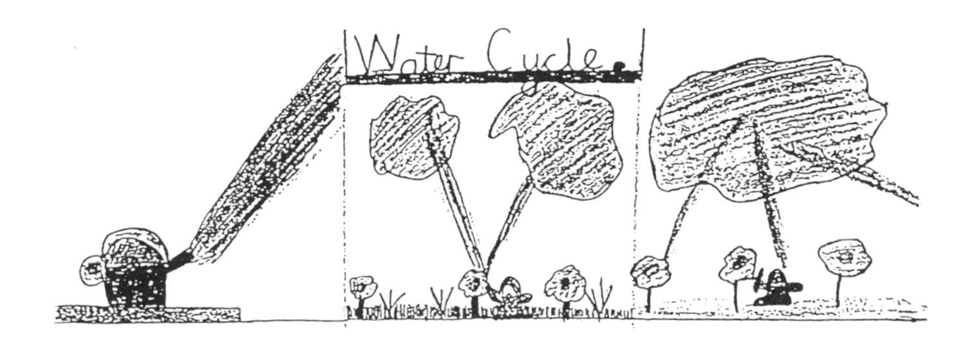

As can be seen in this drawing, the kettle is central to this child's thinking, standing amongst the plants, generating water vapour which streams upwards to form the clouds.

I felt that if the child had stopped to think about this, she would have realized how unlikely it is that the world's fields are full of steaming kettles. Perhaps she would not have, but this incident showed me how ready students are to accept whatever the teacher tells them.

On the other hand, the same children were able to ask me thoughtful questions:

> If the sun makes water evaporate why don't we get more rain in summer than in winter?

Seeing clouds are closer to the sun why don't the water drops in clouds evaporate?
How come we get rain on sunny days?
If dirty water evaporates, why don't we get dirty rain?

So I was convinced that although children's learning is often shallow, and that they often construct strange interpretations of what they hear, they are capable of constructive thinking. I should counter their shallow learning and foster their thinking. But how? What could I do, with my little 8-year-olds, to help them learn with understanding? Whatever I did, it would be based on my assumptions that children learn more effectively when they see links between what they are learning and what they already know; when they link what they learn in school with their experiences outside school; and when they question things they do not understand, the purposes of things they are asked to do in class, and the effectiveness of their own work habits. While many theorists would justify these assumptions, and many classroom teachers would share them, the difficult part is to find a practical way of getting the children to do those things. I thought that thinking books might be the answer.

This was Australia's Bicentenary year, and the media were flooded with accounts of the nation's history. There was much publicity about the 'tall ships', sailing vessels re-enacting the voyage of the First Fleet that came to Australia in 1788. I thought that the children would already know a bit about the First Fleet, and that they would like to learn more. So I chose it for our first topic of the year.

I found that the children were enthusiastic about the tall ships, and indeed many had visited them. All had at least seen them on television. Before long I was talking with them about the First Fleet, and getting them to imagine what it must have been like on those old ships so long ago. Toward the end of the day I gave each of the children a new exercise book. They became excited since they had not used exercise books in the infant department and thought it very grown up. I asked them to label these books 'thinking book'.

'What do you think a "thinking book" might be for?' I asked. Blank faces looked back. I told them they were going to write about things they learnt and that they would need to do lots of thinking to be able to do this. Twenty-one faces still looked blank. I then asked them to write down what they had learnt on that day about the First Fleet and to include any questions they had about things they didn't understand or things they would like to find out more about. I would read these things and write back to them.

This seemed more comprehensible, at least clear enough for all to make their first entries in their new books. They did not take long, as most of them wrote only a few words.

Krysia: 5 February

The First fleet started in 1787. It took them 8 months to sail to Astrailia.

The following day they were all eager to get their books back and read what I had written. I told them that they had to answer any questions I had written in their books before they wrote about the next thing they learnt. Every day they were going to get an opportunity to write in their thinking book about one thing they had learnt. They listened to this, but were more interested in what I had written in their own book than in anything general I had to say.

I had been careful to avoid criticism when I wrote in their books, and had tried to guide them to think about what they had learned. Even so, the first days with the thinking books were frustrating for some who were overwhelmed by being given such an open-ended task; they were used to being given far more guidance when writing. Some of the children felt it was exciting to be treated so maturely and given the responsibility of writing down their own thoughts. Others just had no idea what to do and found the whole thing quite confusing.

After a couple of days I realized why many of the children were having difficulties writing about what they had learnt. They could not see the distinction between what they had done in a particular lesson or activity and what they had learnt by doing it. They simply described the activity in their book.

Allana: 12 April

I learnt at Maths today. We learnt about metres. We hate to write down a Lot of sums. Mrs. Stone hadz a bed of flowers. The flowos had a bed each.

Developing the necessary skills for children to be able to complete the thinking book task was a lengthy process for some. A couple of the children took almost all of first term before they really understood what they were supposed to be reflecting on. This was finally achieved by a combination of conference style discussion between myself and the children and the feedback the children received in their thinking books. For some it meant only one or two reminders to focus on what they learnt rather than what they did.

Kevin: 26 February

At keyboard we just did some stuff that we did last year. At sport we practest our relays because we mite lain the sports.

Kevin, I want you to write about what you have learnt, not what you have done. Do you see the difference?

For some other children this was not enough. They needed to spend some time in order to see the difference between the process and outcome of the activity.

Polly: 16 March

we have to; make a lice blok keepa for keeping the ice blok meting we have to.

What have you learnt by doing this? I don't now whath you are tooking about.

In order to help these children, I arranged 'conferences' similar to the style I use for the children's process writing. During these conferences the children read out their reflections and we discussed them. I asked questions to encourage them to reflect on what they are learning. I taped one such conference, which went as follows:

(After reading the child's reflection.)

Me: So, what have you described in your book?
Polly: About science.
Me: What did you tell me about science?
Polly: What we did with Mr Bullock.
Me: Yes, you've given a good description of what you've done.
Can you remember what I asked you to write about?
Polly: What we learnt in science?
Me: What did you learn in science?
Polly: About ice.
Me: What did you learn about ice?
Polly: Ummm . . . We found out that it melts from the outside, not the inside.
Me: That's interesting. But you haven't written that in your book.
Polly: Oh, no, I didn't.
Me: Can you see that you described what you *did* in your book, not what you *learnt*?
Polly: I think so.
Me: Do you think you can go and write down the things you learnt now?

Fortunately this confusion did not seem to turn the children off thinking books. Those children initially struggling to comprehend the task were still just as excited to get their book back and read what I had written and have another go at writing about what they had learnt.

First Days for Me

The early days for me held much the same range of feelings as the children were experiencing; excitement, frustration, confusion and disappointment. I had not anticipated the trouble some of the children would have in comprehending the task and so had expected a more rapid progress toward achieving the three main objectives I had in mind. I had to make myself step backward and teach those children the skills which were prerequisites to carrying out the task, as I did with Polly in the conference situation.

A couple of the children, however, needed far more basic help with the skills required to carry out the task. These children did not have the language skills needed to write down their reflection in a readable way. One child, Justin, illustrates this point. He arrived at the beginning of the year from Fiji. He was illiterate in English but could speak a limited amount. This made the thinking book exercise impossible for him. He began by dictating his reflections which were restricted by his lack of oral English. He then began to copy things from his own workbook or the chalkboard. Slowly he developed enough confidence to verbalize his first reflection. This did not occur until the fourth week of term.

Justin: 1 March

Today in the maths competiti on I Learnt how to timmes the maths.

Good Justin You learnt your times tables

Gradually he developed adequate language skills to express basic ideas of what he had learnt.

Justin: 11 May

Today I learnt about right angles. I leant how to use the right angles. We learnt once right angles.

This language development occurred through intensive language work involving assistance from the English as a Second Language teacher. Slowly but surely he developed in his understanding of English and his reflections showed similar development in quality.

At the same time there were many unexpected surprises. Some children with quite poor language skills, apparently achieving at quite a low level, showed some surprisingly reflective thinking.

Michelle: 30 March

Today I lent in sicnce that if you can see air you will bamb in to evryiing and you will go to the ring house and raing terdch.

This gave me a real insight into these children that was not evident in their everyday class work.

It was necessary both for my attitude to the task and that of the children to remain positive in my approach. This was difficult when some children did not appear to be making any progress at all. I tried to write positive responses to their reflections while guiding them towards more reflective thinking through questioning.

Polly: 13 April

In Maths I lent horozontle Looks like this —— vertical is this way I Like an l.

Good Polly. I can see that you have already worked out a way to remember which is which.

What use do you think this information may be? If you wont to make a biding and and it is cooked how are peolpe going to live in it? We dont want it like the lening tara pesia. That's very good thinking Polly. I wonder if the person who built the leaning tower of Pisa used a plumb line.

At times, however, they just needed a direct reminder as to what the purpose of the book was.

Krysia: 25 February

Krysia, In this book I don't want you to describe the things you have done, I want you to write down the things that you have learnt. Yeh, ok.

25-2-98 I Learnt today about convicts they had a pretty hard time on the ships.

Chapter Two

Krysia

When Krysia entered our school three years earlier, her mother told the prep grade teacher that she was uncertain about Krysia's grasp of English, since she spoke only Polish at home. The mother spoke English haltingly, with a strong accent. Although Krysia was born in Australia, she had spoken no English until she went to kindergarten. Despite this initial handicap, Krysia quickly showed out in the prep grade. One of the prep children's first tasks was to draw a picture of themselves. Krysia's picture showed great detail, including the checks on her school dress, her name embroidered above her pocket and all the details of her facial features. The teacher was moving around the room, writing dictated sentences on the children's pictures. Krysia, however, said she wanted to write her own. Under her picture Krysia wrote 'here is me in my new school dress'. Although the spelling was 'invented' it was certainly readable. The prep grade teacher and Krysia's teachers in grades 1 and 2 consider her to be above average in ability, particularly in the language area. She does, however, work very slowly and takes a great deal of care over her work. Krysia participates actively in class discussions and regularly asks questions both about things she is interested in and things she doesn't understand.

At the beginning of the thinking books year, I found that Krysia often linked the topics we were talking about with things she had learned before at school and with things she had learned elsewhere. During class discussions she often drew on her own experiences. For example, during a discussion on the First Fleet she talked about visiting the tall ships during the holidays and was interested in how this related to the First Fleet. She asked whether they were the same ships or whether they had followed the same route. This type of linking seemed to be a natural part of her learning style.

Linking was a well-developed aspect of Krysia's learning style, but though she often displayed it in discussions she never used it in her more formal written work. I thought this was a pity, because I believe that the more links people make between the things they know, the richer their understanding. Certainly I encouraged the children to use what they already knew about topics in their writing rather than relying solely on information from books. Krysia's first project on the First Fleet did not include any of the interesting things she had spoken about of her visit to the tall ships. Another project on geography of Australia required the children to take an imaginary trip around the country, answering various questions and commenting on things as they went. I provided them with maps, books, atlases and tourist pamphlets, but also encouraged them to use their own knowledge and experiences. When Krysia came to the section on Central Australia, she was becoming frustrated because the books didn't contain the information she needed. When questioned, however, she said that she had visited Central Australia last holidays and in fact knew the answers to all the questions and plenty of other things as well. She looked surprised when I suggested that she use the things she already knew and said, 'Oh, don't I have to find it in the book then?'

I thought I could use the thinking book to show Krysia that it would be good if she used her out-of-class knowledge in her writing. At first I did not think I would have much trouble with this, since Krysia's first entry in her thinking book revealed she had fully grasped the exercise and its purpose and was confident in putting forward her opinions as well as asking questions about anything she found puzzling.

4 February

I Learnt that: the first fleet arrived in 1788.
When the peple arrived they took away most of the Aboriginies Land and Hunting grounds. They Killed lots of Aboriginies and I rekon it was very crule. There were 11 Ship in the fleet.

I think you have learnt a lot Krysia. Do you have any questions about this work?

Yes I do. Why did they have to kill all those Aboriginics? Can you think of any possible reasons?

Becaus they dident like them.

A few days later, however, she seemed to forget the purposes of the thinking book and was beginning to treat it as a diary. She would have been used to this function as her previous teacher had the children write in a diary every week.

11 February

I had lots of fun with Drawing today. I learnt lots of things with Mr Lysis today at maths It was Realy fun. Vicky came to my house this morrning and we walked together to school.

I was happy that in the early weeks Krysia reflected on what she had learned and asked relevant questions, but she had not yet begun to relate this knowledge with her own experiences or with things she had learnt previously. When I questioned why she did not relate what she had learned to her understanding of real life situations she did not seem to grasp the idea at all and could only relate it to the purposes of that specific activity. This was despite her apparent natural inclination to do this in discussion.

4 March

Why is it important to know how long an iceblock would take to melt? Because in sience we are doing somthing on ice with MR. BUllack

I learnt today about what aborigines wore and why they wore clothes

By yesterdays question, I meant in real life, why would it be useful to know about iceblocks? Because we are doing something with Mr. Bultock on ice.

The only technique I could think of to get Krysia to write about links she saw between what she was learning and real life situations was to write questions in her thinking book, like the one near the end of the 4 March entry, that asked her directly about any links. This had effect, but I remained concerned that her linking was not spontaneous – she remained dependent on me to stimulate her response.

22 March

Can you think of any times in real life that you may need to use subtraction? When I'm lying

Can you think of some different purposes for reading?

likd If your reading your news paper you

would like to know what is happing around the world.

What seemed to be at the root of the problem was Krysia's perception that written work was serious, and had to be restricted to knowledge sanctified by authority – me, the teacher, or books. After all, in discussions she had shown that she formed links easily between school topics and outside experiences, so lack of ability was not the cause. It may be surprising that such a perception could not readily be overcome simply by my telling her that I welcomed use of other knowledge in written work, but then we need to appreciate that Krysia built up the perception over several years of life, in school and at home. One of the messages I learned from the thinking books is that it takes time and persistence to change perceptions. Part of that time and persistence goes in building up confidence and trust.

The encouragement I gave Krysia in the thinking book to write about links eventually convinced her that it was acceptable to include out-of-school purposes and accounts of her experiences in projects and in the thinking book itself, as I saw in her 13 April entry.

13 April

Today, I learnt about horizontal and Vertical. Horizontal is ——— and Verti-cal is |. My friends have got a Etch a scetch.

On it, it has two
knobs and one says
Vertical and the other is
Horizontal. If I'm building.
a House I will know
wich is Vertical and
Horizontal.

Many of the potential uses that Krysia saw for what she learned remained bound to school. Her 20 April entry illustrates how she thought about learning as something to satisfy authority, in a test.

20 April

I might need to
know how to spell it when
lim writing.

I'm sure you will. What would happen if
you didn't know how to spell properly?

When I have children and
they have a big spelling
test and They ask you how
to spell it, and you tell it

to them wrong and then
they will drop out of the.
test.

It was difficult to overcome Krysia's perception that written work should not draw on outside experiences, without becoming critical or judgmental about her reflections. I knew, however, that inclusion of criticisms and corrections would destroy the thinking books, so I continued to encourage Krysia to bring together facts from books and outside experiences. Slowly this had effect.

17 May

Today I learnt about Australian
animals. I alrcady knew how a
baby kangaroo was born, becausе
I saw it on the David Johnston
collection. I also learnt how
Kangaroos balance on there tails
and kick each other when they
fight. I have been to a Safari
park and have seen two
Kangaroos fight. When they stand
up they are bigger than my
dad. I wonder what they feel
like when. there born.

In the middle of the year I asked Krysia whether the thinking books had helped her learning. She said, 'They've helped me to spell better and they've helped me because I'm a better thinker now. I answer questions better too. I used to just answer questions with one word, now I think about it and write more sentences.' Her response is impressive for an 8-year-old, but I note that she does not mention bringing in out-of-school experiences in her writing. Krysia is an able girl, whom most teachers would rate as a successful student. I do, too, but even able students can improve. The thinking book brought out Krysia's lack of linking in written work and was the means of helping her to overcome that.

Chapter Three

Learning Together

I have found that I learn most effectively when I am working cooperatively with others. Listening stimulates ideas, and then in order to share these thoughts with others I am forced to make them clear to myself. The others' comments bring about further revision, and extensions. Because I had found this experience so helpful, I wanted to give the children in my class opportunities to work together. I thought that would enhance their learning as well as promote their social skills.

In the second week of school I introduced cooperative learning. I put the children into groups that I had thought about carefully. Each group contained mixed abilities. I gave the groups an interesting problem: after I had read to them Eric Carle's story *The Very Hungry Caterpillar*, each group had to represent, using any of the various materials I provided, the quantity of food the caterpillar ate on each day of the week. The children were familiar with the story (though they still liked to have it read to them). I thought the task simple enough for every child to be involved, while it allowed scope for each group to make its own decisions and produce something unique.

I watched the groups at work. My first discovery was that children do not work together easily. Although all the groups but one ended with a reasonable product, none worked in a way that satisfied me.

In the group that did not complete the task, Tim and Krysia argued for almost the whole time about how to begin.

At length Tim withdrew in a huff because more of the group supported Krysia than him. He sat slightly apart, loudly disclaiming any responsibility for the finished product, which he asserted was going to be 'weak'. By the time he withdrew, Krysia and the others had only a few minutes to complete a half-hour task.

Things were not so dramatic in the other groups, but there was little effective cooperation in them either. In each group one or two children took control and gave others menial tasks such as colouring in headings, ruling sheets, or fetching things. Some children just sat and watched. I asked Alice, one of the watchers, what her group was doing. She said, 'making things'. She appeared to have no notion of what the group was trying to make, let alone contributing to it or giving it any direction.

This was not what I had planned. I had assumed, wrongly, that the children had the skills necessary for working together and learning effectively through cooperation.

I thought about how I might overcome this difficulty. I had established the thinking books to encourage the children to see purpose in their learning, so that they would have more control over it and would gain better understanding of what they learned. Perhaps I could use the thinking books to improve their cooperation and teach them to take effective and responsible roles in group work.

I began by discussing with the children the purposes of working cooperatively. I asked them to suggest why it is important to work well together. They responded with numerous reasons: minimizing arguments, keeping the teacher happy, keeping the noise level down so the teacher next-door won't complain. All of these initial suggestions concerned the working atmosphere in the classroom; none touched on direct help with learning, such as the sharing of ideas or helping each other to understand. I tried to get the children to think about how they might help each other learn, then asked them to write in their thinking books what they had learned about how they learned best. Most entries showed that the children thought they learned best by working quietly alone.

Nicole

I work best when ~~I'm~~ it's quite and when I'm in pafnals and when I'm thinkin g

I suspected that this belief reflected their conditioning in earlier grades. Most teachers encourage and reward this style of learning. The belief made it harder to get the children to value cooperative learning.

In our next class discussion I encouraged the children to think about cooperation outside the classroom. I asked them to think about times in the world outside when they would need to cooperate with others. This was effective; they began to see real purpose in cooperation. Tim talked at length about the need to cooperate on the football field and what happens when someone 'hogs' the ball (I suspect that he had been given this lecture by his football coach). Vicky spoke about how her stepfather was put off work for having a fight with his boss. Many of the children related stories of family members needing to cooperate in order to achieve something. I spoke about the value of working with other teachers, sharing ideas and resources. The children seemed to appreciate the point much more in this discussion than in the previous one.

I asked the children to reflect again on what they had learned about cooperation. Their thinking book entries revealed a broader and clearer understanding of the advantages of working together.

Nicole

I lent about cowoperating that you make more friends and you lean things by lisning.

If you dont cowoperat in teams your team loses

At first I was not sure that the children would link the outside-world advantages of cooperation with what they did in the classroom, but I soon found that they did. Apparently they needed to see the general value and purpose of working together, and then could apply it to sharing ideas, questioning each other, sharing classroom tasks and developing a group product. Being told to cooperate was not enough; they first had to understand its value as an aid to learning.

Later in the year when we were working on a large unit about the Olympic Games, I again got the children to work in mixed ability groups. Their task was to investigate a question suggested by one group: Do people with bigger feet run faster? I soon saw that the children had come far since their first attempt at group work. In every group the children huddled together, discussing how they would solve the problem. Although not all contributed ideas, all appeared to be involved and to know what their group was doing. The finished product was not much better than that of the earlier effort, but I think the learning was better.

From time to time during the year I asked the children to write in their thinking books what they had learned during group work. I encouraged them to reflect not only on the information they acquired but also on what they had learned about working together. This helped them to understand the purpose of learning, and some of the actions that made it easier to learn better.

Chapter Four

Ariana

Ariana's parents were born in Egypt, of Greek origin. They are active Jehovah's Witnesses, and do not allow Ariana to participate in nationalistic ceremonies such as flag-raising assemblies or any special celebrations such as children's birthdays, Christmas, Easter and Anzac Day. Nor is she allowed a blood transfusion if the need arises nor to take part in competitive sport. When Ariana was in prep grade she fell from a piece of climbing equipment and cut her leg which bled profusely. She became hysterical, screaming that her 'mummy said she wasn't allowed to have blood'.

Ariana's previous teachers considered her to be average in academic ability although lacking in creativity. At the beginning of our year together I found her rather nervous – she often chewed her fingernails, frowned frequently, and cried readily when the other children teased her.

Ariana was anxious about the main topic we were studying in first term, the history of Australia. She asked frequently whether she was allowed to learn anything about Australia, and suggested that she had better not take part. When the topic had been approved by her older brother she did agree to learning something of it, but remained unenthusiastic.

For some weeks Ariana took no part in class discussions, and did the bare minimum of written work. She never asked a question or showed any interest in any topic.

Like the rest of her written work, Ariana's first entries in her thinking book were minimal, and displayed her lack of understanding.

4 February

200 years ago Captain Hook invented AustraLIA

Although she seemed to have some notion of the purpose of the book, she seemed unable to reflect on what she had learned.

10 February

Today I want tell you some thing that I have leant

After a couple of weeks, in which I spoke with her about learning and what she might write in her book, her entries got longer but she had not grasped the purpose. She described what she had done, not what she had learned. I pointed this out to her, but she continued to miss the distinction between doing and learning.

23 February

Today in my project we had to write about Aborigines and we had to make a picture

29 February

IN Mr. BULLOCKS GROUP
we have to make ice
What did you learn Ariana?
A Lot
I want you to write down exactly
what you did learn Ariana.

4 March

today in Science we had to
put coffee, sugar, and more
things to see if they will
melt and if it dose not
melt then you are good
at it.

When the entries in the thinking book did not improve, I decided that Ariana should do them orally, in private discussion with me. She then did appear to grasp the difference between what she had done and what she had learned, for although she said little she was able to state one thing she had learned in the lesson. I asked her to write that in her thinking book. Her next entry gave me hope that we had broken through, since it stated what she had learned as well as what she was doing.

8 March

Today I Leant that we have to keep in time. Next week we have to think of our own dance.

Further difficulties lay ahead. Although from this point on Ariana began each entry with 'Today I learnt . . .', she went on to describe the things she had done or was to do.

17 March

Today in Sport I Leant that we had to jump over the ball

21 March

Today I Leant that we had to fine things on a Sheet and I liked it

In my written responses I pointed out to Ariana that she was still describing actions rather than what she learned from them, but I had no effect until I spoke again with her. Together we read each of her entries, and then I asked Ariana each time, 'What do you think the teacher might have wanted you to learn?' This made sense to her. Her next entry combined a brief description of the activity with what she had learned.

12 April

Today I leant we had to ~~to~~ fine places and I found I leant some new places and some more places. I leant how to get to Canberra.

From then on Ariana always managed to write about something she had learned, though for some time her entries remained brief and did not refer to any links with things she already knew or with her experiences. Nor did she ask any questions in her book. Although I encouraged Ariana, through written responses and questions, to think about the purposes of activities and relate them to out-of-school situations, she found that difficult. She could relate the purposes of activities only with other learning.

15 April

Today I leant ~~that we had~~ how to sepll definitely and I liked it Why is it good to learn how to spell properly? Then you can Spell it properly. Why is that useful? I do not kown

My responses in her book continued to praise her for stating what she had learned. I also asked her to write about times she might have used that knowledge, but she usually ignored these requests or gave glib answers.

Early in May one of her entries did at last link some learning with a potential use of it. My response attempted to reinforce this linking. I hoped that Ariana would see it as a positive thing to do and would be encouraged to continue doing it.

2 May

Today I leant how to do new sums I can use it if someone wants to lean. at school and if you want to fine a price.

That's... very good thinking Ariana. I often need to use sums to work out how much things cost and whether. I have enough money.

That 2 May entry did indeed mark a watershed in Ariana's schoolwork. From that point she made an effort to link learning with experiences and uses. She did not ask any questions through her thinking book, but her entries showed more interest in the things she learned.

16 May

Today I learnt how to use
the alfabetticle odder but for
the Gold Rush. I have used the
alfabetticle odder to fired some
thing in the dictionery.

17 May

Today I learnt that when
some anamails have a
baby it is pink and the
birds when they have a baby
it is Yellow. I already
Knew about the bird and
it is very intnteresting

Throughout the first term Ariana had a negative feeling about writing in the thinking book. When I handed the books out she often screwed up her nose, and she was always slow to get her pencils organized before writing. After the 2 May entry her attitude changed. She often brought her book to me so that I could read it before she handed it in, asking 'Am I getting better?' or making a comment such as 'I was really thinking today'.

Although Ariana is much more positive about school, there has been no miraculous change. She still participates rarely in discussions, and never asks questions in class. She does, though, recognize that the thinking book helped her learning. She told me 'They have helped me a bit in talking about things and learning. Sometimes they help me to remember things.' I believe that the book did improve the quality of Ariana's learning, but whether she will continue to think about the purpose of lessons and what school has to do with life outside is far from certain. It will depend on the encouragement she gets from her future teachers.

Chapter Five

Learning to Question

When I taught infant classes I was bombarded constantly with questions about all kinds of things; from those relevant to classroom activities to some quite unrelated to anything happening at school. Yet the level of question asking dwindles quickly as children progress through school. After just a couple of years at school children seem to learn that questions are for teachers to ask and children to answer, not vice versa.

The behaviour of the children in this class at the beginning of the year certainly confirmed this observation. In class discussions they were, with few exceptions, quite passive. They tended not to question anything they did not understand, preferring to copy someone who understood the directions or to wait passively until I gave further guidance. After explaining a classroom activity, I always encouraged children to ask if there was something they didn't understand. At the beginning of the year, this encouragement rarely got a response. I often would find, however, that many of the children didn't understand what was expected of them. They were reluctant to ask for help.

Similarly, the children had difficulty in posing questions about any topic on which we were working. Even when their interest level was high and they had some background knowledge in the area, they struggled to form questions to investigate the topic. They appeared to see asking questions as the teacher's role and theirs to answer them. When I asked them to think about what they wanted to find out and to write down any questions they had about the first topic to be investigated for the year, Australia's Bicentenary, I saw many blank and puzzled faces.

Almost half wrote nothing, unsure of what to write. This worried me, for I had long believed that asking questions is a fundamental part of learning.

One of the objectives I had set out for the use of thinking books was that of active learning through questioning. I hoped that the children would begin to question things they did not understand, things that interested them, the purposes of classroom activities and the effectiveness of their own work habits.

At the beginning of the year I could see that this objective was not going to be easy to attain, since not only did few children write questions but also those who did formed simple factual ones like those in a trivia quiz. Questions such as 'When did Captain Cook discover Australia?' and 'How many convicts came out on the First Fleet?' were common. The children had no real interest in finding out the answers to such questions – they were merely asking them for the sake of completing a task.

I thought about all the things that discourage children from asking questions. Perhaps they had been derided by their peers or a teacher, or criticised for not knowing the answer or for not listening carefully to instructions. Perhaps they had found that their questions were not taken seriously, or never got answered. Perhaps they were just too shy to speak up in the formal school setting. Perhaps they could not think quickly enough to frame a question. I thought that the thinking books might overcome these inhibitions. They would provide a way for the children to ask questions that was personal but not face-to-face or public. They would give the children time to think of how to express themselves. And perhaps most important of all, I could give positive feedback, showing the children that I valued their questions, either by writing responses in the books or by using the questions in class.

I intended to develop the children's asking of questions through more activities than just the thinking books. I planned to use their questions as a springboard for discussions and investigations. I would have the children's questions typed up early into the study of a particular topic and allow them to select which questions they would like to discuss or investigate. I felt it was important for them to see that their questions were valued and encouraged. I would give time to all genuine questions – either noting them for later attention or handling them on the spot. I could see that this group of children needed such immediate feedback to encourage and stimulate question asking.

I found that the children appreciated a genuine response to their questions. At the beginning of the year I was providing positive feedback for their questions through written comments such as 'good question' in their thinking books. After a while this didn't seem enough. The best feedback I could give was a genuine, personal response or to use their questions. To add the question to a class list for investigation or to use it during a class discussion really seemed to emphasize the importance of questioning and to demonstrate the role questions played in learning. Understanding and valuing the purpose behind question-asking through really using the children's questions stimulated a lot more effort and a better quality of question being asked. It seemed that my understanding and valuing of the importance of questioning was not enough, it had to have meaning and purpose for the children too.

The development of a personal interaction with myself was an important aspect of their questions. Many of the children used their thinking books to find out my opinions on issues or to ask about my experiences.

Tim: 8 February

Wero did the first Fleet
Stop 1st and 2nd?
have you been on a bout?

Early in the year I discussed types of questions with the children. I pointed out that all but one of the first set they had written had a simple right or wrong answer. They were fact questions. The unusual one was more complicated, we had to think about it before we could answer it, and there were several possible answers. Since we only had one 'thinking' question, as a group we generated a few more. The children soon discovered that these questions tended to start with Why? How? and What if?

I expected that the private nature of the book would allow the children to take the greater amount of risk involved in framing thinking questions as against factual ones. That did happen, though not as frequently as I had hoped until late in the year. At first they tended to ask factual questions about something that interested them and that they wanted to know more about.

Kevin: 4 February

When the first fleet came in 1788 and when they stoppe-d at botany bay and they steped on to the land and when they saw the animal-s were they fritend of them or they not afrade.

Perhaps if you imagine yourself in their situation Kevin, you could guess how they might have felt.

They might of thiked they were going to shoot them. They SHO-ot some and capturdd. some some captives fell over boar wile they were comeing to Australia and why was it called Australia?

Some of their questions about content concerned complex social issues, and revealed the children's empathy with the historical people they were learning about.

Jenny: 3 March

What questrons do you have about our work on abrorigines?

why did the wite people spole the abrignies life? and why did the wite men take all of Australia? Mrs Swan I feal sorry for the abrigrines Is ther same way we can help?

The number of questions written at the beginning of each topic to be studied grew steadily. The style of questions changed also. They became genuine thinking questions which the children were interested in rather than the pointless trivial questions asked at the beginning of the year. A lot of reflection and thought was beginning to go into the questions as the children were aware I would value and respond thoughtfully to them.

About mid-way through the year we planned a unit on the Olympic Games. I asked the children to list all the things they would like to find out about the Games. Instead of the blank or puzzled faces I'd seen earlier in the year they all put their heads down and wrote. After about ten minutes I asked for their questions. Most children had written at least eight questions related to the topic. All were keen to read their own aloud and this sharing of questions naturally triggered many more. Each of their questions was then discussed and put into a category for later investigation or discussion. There was an atmosphere of excitement. The children were keen to make sure the study of the topic would help them find answers to their questions.

The early days of encouraging question asking through the thinking books had paid off. The early experiences had been instrumental in establishing this atmosphere of thriving question asking.

The children also used their thinking books to question things they didn't understand in class. They did not always pose these reflections as questions but were still able to identify the things that had confused them in class.

Catherine: 13 April

Today in myths were horizo Lins and Verticl I am hiring the [illegible] two Lins So mach that I am biging to geting canfuosd. Look to the hrisn and it will rmind you.

Stephanie: 13 May

PROBLEMSOLVING

Today in Problemsolving I lornt how to write
1000 but in numbers. once I saw how to
do 1000 I said to my self "Ah now I've got the
hole ider. Mr Lises tuld us this story abot
when he was small how he lornt
to cont. ~~Now~~ I thort you did 1012
like this 10012. When Mr Lises said "Dose
eneywon know how to wrt in numbers
1012 I put my hand up I was
abot to say yes I know 10012 But
he did not pick me. I lornt how to
make Slome sapes out of sqwers. I lornt
alot.

The children believed that I would help them with the things they wrote that they did not understand, either through my responses in their thinking books or through additional assistance in the next lesson, but found it easier to write about these difficulties than to frame them into questions. Similarly, early in the year they tended to comment on the purposes of classroom activities rather than to question them. As time went by, however, when they could not see the point of something they began to write more and more questions about it. Often these questions were forceful, and incorporated alternatives for me to think about.

Paul: 20 June

What is the porpse of doing morning talk? It wastest time So does exercises. I ~~to~~ learnt how to long Durvson with remaunder and normal remaundes. Why don't we ~~even~~ ever do pucuacion and languge?
Now I see why we have show and tell. Why do we have silent reading? Why don't we just read out loud? I enjoyed working on kilometers and recorder. Why do we have recorder. Why don't we play the vilin. Why is it importent to bring a noval. Why not picture story book.

The questions about purpose showed that the children believed that each classroom activity should have a function that they understood. I suspect that that belief may not be universally common in schools, or even universities. These 8-year-olds became skilled at determining the value of each activity and each piece of content.

Jenny: 22 April

today we had spelling
and I lirent that if
you don't lirn how to spell
then when you write letters
people will not under stand
you and if you are a ~~se~~
secrtery well you will
need to know how to spell
other wise you will be
fierd... bang

The extent to which they developed in questioning purpose in lessons became obvious early the following year after they had moved on to another teacher. After just a couple of days with this group of children their new teacher approached me in the staff room with 'Didn't those kids drive you crazy last year? They question everything, even what I do! Why are we doing this? What is the purpose of that?'

There was one aim in which I was less successful than I had hoped. I wanted the children to reflect on their learning styles and work habits, but this occurred only rarely. Sometimes they used their thinking books to make excuses for failing to learn, but they never formed these reflections into questions about work habits.

Ariana: 9 March

Today I wanted to finish in time
but I didet because... I was
to slow. What made you slow?
I was talking to much

Catherine: 10 March

I am afrad I didn't
lern erey theink abuie
Abrigany becas I yosd
my won nolig it mast
be a big disapintmant
ps I am soye my riting isnt so good
I got the nolig from THE
WERLD ARANDAS,
famy and frens.

Although they did not write questions about learning style or work habits, when after four months I asked the children to reflect on what they had learned from writing in their thinking books, most showed a good understanding.

Jenny: 27 May

Today Mrs swan asked us
to write in our thinking
books what we lirent by
doing our thinking books
and I Lirent that you
give us our thinking
books because you think
that it is inportnt that
we do some thinking
in sted of lirning nothing
well we do lirn something but we
just don't think of What we
lirn and you wont us
to think so that you
know what we lirn
and that arfter all
is a very inportnt
thing don't you thin
k Mrs swan I think
it is very inportent.

Kevin: 27 May

I have been learning by writeing in my thinking book how to think a lots more harder and think into the future for what use it might be and also thinking about when you have use it And answering quitions and writing quitions down.

Stephanie: 27 May

I think thinking books are great I think they help me think. And pluse. they I mean you know what i domit And they are, well. ereytime they they are fun in or of lots of ways and they help me spell, help me think and help me read, but i really don't have troble reading only if well only sometims if i am reading TV week

Chapter Six

Anna

Anna's parents were born in Greece, and though she and her two older brothers attended our school since prep grade her father speaks only a minimal amount of English and her mother none at all. Greek language and culture are important to Anna's family. The three children attend Greek school on Saturdays. Their parents give them a lot of help with their Greek studies. They told the teacher of one of the boys that Greek school was more important than their children's regular schooling. The Greek school teachers considered all three children to be high achievers.

At our school Anna is one of the quietest children. She prefers quiet games with dolls and toys to energetic playground contests, and is seldom seen running. She gets on well with other children, especially other Greek girls in the class. Friends invite her to their birthday parties, but her parents do not allow her to attend.

In class, Anna does not participate much in discussions. She rarely asks for help, and seldom speaks to me about anything not associated with school. Her written work, like her physical appearance, is extremely neat. Mistakes and untidiness upset her. If she makes a mistake with her work she prefers to begin all over again on fresh paper to fixing the error. One time she was working on a large sheet of project paper on native animals. She had put about three hours work into the project and it was well on the way. She was ruling a line when she was bumped. The ruler moved and the line was crooked. She insisted that she wanted to begin the project all over again rather than to fix up the crooked line. Unlike most of the other children, who will try at anything,

Anna usually waits and looks around at what people are doing before she begins it herself. This delay is not a problem because when she does begin she works quickly, and is usually one of the first to finish.

Anna's previous teachers rated her above average in basic skills of reading, spelling and arithmetic, especially in her automatic response to number facts, but lacking in imagination and problem-solving ability. Her work at the beginning of the year confirmed this judgment. Little of her writing was original, mostly stories she had read or heard from other children or from fairytales. When I encouraged her to write some things from her own experiences, it became clear that part of her difficulty was that she had an uneventful life. Apart from Greek school, the only people she sees on weekends are her family and relatives. Since her parents do not drive a car the family makes few outings. Anna cannot recall ever being away on a holiday other than to stay with her cousins.

When I asked Anna about the things she did at home, she described helping her mother with housework and cooking, playing with her brothers and watching television. She seemed to spend a lot of time passively watching television.

Although Anna's early entries in her thinking book showed that she was more aware than most of the children what she was supposed to do, they generally lacked evidence of real thought. Her first entry was longer than that of most of the children, but recapitulated part of what I told them rather than introduced a new idea or problem. This entry also is one of several that showed that the children confused Captains Phillip, Cook and Hook (which I discuss in chapter 9). It also contains the same notion as Ariana's, that Hook invented Australia. I do not know whether Anna got these ideas from other children or whether she was their source, but it would be consistent with her other behaviour for her to be a receiver rather than an originator.

4 February

Before white people were here in Australio
there were aboriginis. Then Captain Hook
came with captives to Austalia.
Who was the aboriginis captain?
Captain Hook inveted Australia
There were eleven Ship in the first
fleet.

I encouraged the children to write in their thinking books any questions they had about the topic. It took some weeks for many to learn how to do this. Anna wrote questions from the start, but usually they were trite, as though she were adding a token question because I required one. She showed no interest in finding the answers to any of her questions.

18 February

Because the books right .it. How much
brothers did Captain Hook have an the
11 ships? How old was Captain Hook when
he was sailing on the boat?

Perhaps Anna's asking of questions as a routine without deep thought was connected with her unwillingness to take risks. In all her school work she tried hard to get things right, that is to find out what I wanted as the answer. Late in second term I gave the children some mathematics problems of a type they had not encountered before, so that I could discuss with them ways of solving the problems. Anna was upset by this, and would not attempt an activity of which she was unsure. She was reluctant to accept that there could be more than one correct method of solution.

All year Anna was concerned about not making mistakes, though she gradually became more tolerant of corrections she could make to her own work. Her entries for 8 and 9 June, later in this chapter, contain crossings out that would have upset her in February.

Although Anna remained more cautious than most of her classmates, her thinking book showed a lot of change in her approach to learning. At first Anna used the book more as a means of communication with me than an aid to reflect on her own learning. Many of her questions asked for my opinions on a topic.

29 February

I leant that they felt or kind of things. Anyone can die easaly. The conuits had to work relly had or they whould get whiped How would you fill Mrs. Swan? I would of felt terrible, lonly, and hungry

Slowly this began to lead to a barrage of questions about what I did when I was at school. Every lesson or topic the children were asked to reflect on, Anna would include in her reflection a question as to when I did this when I was at school.

30 March

30 March Today I learnt some more times. Thank you Mrs. Swan for teaching some more clock times. When did you learnt to do your clocks?

Although Anna may have realized that questions about me had little relation to the purpose of the thinking book, she sneaked them in anyway.

28 March

Here is an agsanple what whant to tell you. You always put the 5 or the ather numbers up to nine on the right side Me and Krysia put it on the left side. We were silly duffers. When you were small did you do maths alott and it was relly hard? Today some people thought it was hard. For me it was isy What was your mum's and dad's name? What name would you like the best? I wish my name was Suzan it would of been nice.

19 April

Today I learnt in Sport how to ceep in time with the music. Next week Mrs. Cowll said you haft to make up a dance with four people in it. Me, Elizabeth, Ariana and Krysia a going to do a dance together. Mrs. Cowll thinks they are going to be terrifick so do I. When did you learnt to dance Mrs. Swan?

For a long time I believed that Anna was writing these questions simply as a formula, but at length it became clear that she really was interested in the answers.

8 June

Today at sharing I learnt how to share ideas. I also learnt to not be a bosy boots because other people want something to do. I remember doing this last year but with words. I think nesct time I do it I will do it better. I have youst it last year. When you where small did you do this? Everything you have learnt us have you learnted it when you where small?

Anna wanted to know how I decided what they were going to learn. Did I just teach them all the things I learned when I was at school, or did I get my ideas elsewhere? This led to an interesting class discussion on who should decide what things should be taught at school and why.

As time passed, Anna began to relate the things she was learning with life outside our present classroom. At first she found it difficult to think of anything other than future learning ('hiscall' – high school):

25 March

Can you think of any times when you
might need to use those sums ~~s~~ in
your life? Provbly at hiscall but march
more harder then now. Today. I
learnt how to Subturact. When you were
in hiscall was it hard? Or eseay?

At first Anna would only try to connect what we were learning with other experiences when I wrote a question in her book. Later, when she had understood what I wanted, Anna added real life applications for the things they were learning without further prodding from me. Sometimes she even invented applications when there was no real purpose other than fantasy. The gun she refers to in the next entry is a large cannon. This is a much more imaginative notion than she seemed capable of at the beginning of the year.

11 May

I also learnt at Sovereign Hill how
to shoot the gun that they
youst at Sovereign Hill a long
time ago. It will be yous/ull for
me because if someone court
me I will set ~~the~~ the gun so
I can shoot them.

Gradually, Anna's entries began to show real reflection about the use of what she was learning.

9 June

Today I leart in Spelling how to spell some words that I didint now. It will be a lot of yous to me because when I can wright to my pen. freind and I got to make shore that I have got no rongs in it. I've youst it ~~at~~ home when me and my brother play school.

While some other children may have had more progress than Anna through the thinking books, she moved a long way during the year from the passive, unreflecting state she was in at the start. Although she was then classed as one of the more able students, it was an ability to conform, to cope with direct tasks in which there was a correct method and a correct answer. I believe that the thinking book rounded out Anna's learning, by opening to her the need to ponder, to see what the learning was for, and to be more ready to think about open questions. When I asked Anna half-way through the year how writing in the thinking book had helped her, she said 'They've helped me to think hard every day. I ask a lot of questions about things now.'

Chapter Seven

Arthur

Arthur is a very little boy, the youngest in the class, extremely small and thin for his age. His parents emigrated from Greece before he and his two brothers – one younger, one older – were born. The parents are reasonably fluent in English, though they speak only Greek at home. Since Arthur began at the school in prep grade, he and his family have been to Greece twice for extended holidays. Arthur spent more than half of his grade 2 year in Greece.

Arthur's previous teachers considered him to be immature in his social behaviour and in his progress in learning, and classed him as below average in ability. He does not mix well with the children in his grade. At recess times I used to see him playing with one or two younger children, but even then he preferred creative play to physical games or ball activities. When he was in the prep grade he often played with dolls or in the dress-up corner where he was involved in 'make-believe' play. This year he spends most of his recess time in adventure-type play with model cars and animals in the sand pit.

When I ask Arthur to work cooperatively with a group, he does not contribute to the making of decisions. He always takes a minor role usually involving art work on the group's presentation. During these sessions he often asks whether he may work on his own.

During free activity time in a class, when most children choose to play games from the games trolley, Arthur almost always uses the time to write stories or to work on pictures to illustrate his stories. He has written many stories this year, all imaginative and unusual. The themes are usually a fantasy, such as the set he titled *Cheesesticks in Space* which are about different types of cheese fighting in space. He has written also a number of stories about his sole survival after the world blows up. Not all of his stories involve aggression or disaster.

Arthur enjoys art, and demonstrates some talent. Like his stories, his artwork never has the stereotyped images that are common in children's drawings. He draws machinery and robots rather than trees, houses and flowers.

Arthur rarely finishes set work in formal activities such as mathematics and language lessons. I found his behaviour in one of these sessions interesting. He did not listen while I told the children what to do, but went happily to his table to begin. He opened his book and looked at the board, when he saw the heading which he copied onto the top of his page. Then he decorated the heading with his coloured pencils. He spent quite a bit of time at this, then got a piece of cardboard from his locker. He cut a strip from it and wrote 'Arthur's bookmark' on it, and began to decorate it. It was not long before another child at his table called out 'Arthur isn't working, he's making a bookmark.' Arthur looked up, quite unperturbed, and began to copy what the boy next to him had written. But before long he stopped copying and began to write his own words, in which he deviated a little from the instructions.

Many of Arthur's reflections in his thinking book early in the year were, like much of his classroom work, only distantly related to the activity he had been asked to write on, and usually were brief.

10 February

The same people died from the trip and they did not get lots of food.

16 February

If they dun snwthink bad They got wept

What else did you learn Arthur?

They died from geting wept

At times his entries had nothing at all to do with the given topic, or were related to only a minor point.

9 March

I waterd for Miis Gaceo so I can reid her my story it is colde The piece from the car that turned into a robot man.

21 April

Today I lernt haw you will fell if you went arond. Australia. in a car. or in a bus or are tran.

How would you feel?

sick.

I was conscious that I should be careful not to damage Arthur's creativity if I attempted to make him focus more on the lessons. But something had to be done, since he often drew incorrect conclusions from the minor pieces of information he picked up during a lesson. Some of these errors occurred because he ignored the context of the lesson.

30 March

At easter you get lots of chocolet eggs and lots of babys get born.

Why are babies born at Easter Arthur? Becose we becein a new life.

Arthur's capacity for divergent thinking used to show up in class discussions as well as in his thinking book. He does not participate often, but when he does he frequently picks up a small aspect and follows a different line from the original focus of the discussion. This has a good side, of course, since we do not want totally subservient and convergent learning, but often led Arthur to mix fact with fiction. The next extract shows some of that mix.

6 May

I lerant obot usin maps to us them cefolle & to no the roods and dont meoks them up wiht the rall wae tracks

That's good Arthur: What would happen if you mixed up roads with railway lines?

You will not go were you won't to go or you will be on the railway lines and if your are on the railwaylines a tran will crach into your car.

Another example of Arthur's predilection for minor, side issues occurred on our excursion to Sovereign Hill, a rebuilt goldfields town. We had been studying the nineteenth century gold rushes as a part of the history of Australia. The children seemed to learn much about life on the goldfields from this excursion, but in his thinking book Arthur focussed on a teacher's passing comment about the use of lavender bags.

11 May

What I Learnt

Yesterday wen Grad 3S 4L 3/4.B went to Sovereign Hill. I went in an clase that they had wen Sovereign Hill had in the oldin days and " Vicky had to drees up like an oldinday Girl and Jason had to drees up like an oldinday boy and. At the end wen we had to leave we maket lavada bags and the ladys put the lavada bag ander there dress. Because the ladys olny have a barth onee a year and the lavada bag keep them from smaleng.

That's right Arthur. I still don't think they would have smelt very nice. What do we do with lavendar bags today? Today they used lavenderbag from putting they lavendbags in there cabets so no enceas do not eat the close

Yes Arthur. Is your mum using her lavendar bag for this? No she dose not like the small of the Lavender bag so she frode it away in the rabes bin.

While Arthur's penchant for the odd event or for fantasy has its charm, and certainly should not be suppressed, it needs to be balanced by an ability to perceive the purpose of an activity. If all that Arthur was going to get out of third grade was skill at decorating bookmarks and a collection of unrelated facts such as the use of lavender bags, I feared that his knowledge was not going to fit together and further up in the school he would fall behind the other children. So in my written questions and comments in his book I tried to get him to recognize the reason why we had particular lessons. It took a while for me to recognize that this was desirable, and of course longer still for Arthur to change. It was not until second term that Arthur began to reflect on his learning style and to think about what he was learning and to use it outside the classroom.

18 May

Today at Queck swams
I remender haw to do ÷
because i all was ceep
on forgeting. I remember
because i sae that looks
lick the haw many sen

7 June

Today in the maths
conpiticon i Learnt an
eisa way to do my
times tabols.

When i have used it.
I have used il wen
my dad. told my to go
to the milk bar and
he told me to get tow
packets of sagars. one
for his werck and
one for the house.
and i had to multtipli
them.

As Arthur began to think more about the activity and to concentrate on instructions, he became greatly excited about school. He often asked if he could show the Principal his work and began to take his books home to show his parents. When other teachers visited the classroom, Arthur would be right by their side showing his work. He seemed to be both pleased with and surprised at himself.

With success in class, Arthur began to change his entries in his thinking book. Spontaneously he organized his reflections under headings. When I asked him why he set out his book in this way, he said it was so he could remember all the things to think about and to help him write them. His first heading said simply, 'What I learnt.'

20 May

What i learnt

Today i learnt how to do the toretow diving into the water. I don it the dest and i dow it warm we do not packtes siwmming and. I don the freest-il the best

That's good Arthur. Why is it useful to learn to swim? If you are in danger at the beach wen you are in water so. You cood be safe. That's why you shod now haw to siwm.

Later Arthur added the heading 'What use it may be', probably because of my responses to his reflections when I often wrote 'What use do you think learning this might be?' But the idea of a heading itself was Arthur's own.

26 May

Today in mofes I leant an easier way to do ÷.

What was the easier way Arthur?
8÷2=4
Today in libirer i lent how to do a domino story and I rowt Wen I went to the bech.
What use it mae be.
So wen i grow up i could macke up a domino story by mis sillf

More and more headings appeared: 'When I have Used It Before', 'When I Have Seen It Before', 'What I Already Knew About It', and 'My Questions'. I was struck by the maturity of these headings; all were appropriate, and assisted Arthur to link what he was learning with his experiences in the world and with his prior knowledge. He had come a long way from the little boy who picked up an occasional bright pebble from a lesson.

The projects Arthur did early in the year were barely related to the given topic and contained incorrect information. He frequently just invented things to write into projects, and did not appear to understand that some work required accurate information. I had encouraged the children to use their own knowledge rather than copying slabs of information from books, but where I had had difficulty convincing Krysia of this Arthur had accepted it to the extent of interpreting it as a charge to make up his own knowledge. All this changed gradually along with the change in his thinking book entries, until his projects in late second term contained interesting information that was well organized and that related directly to the topic.

Arthur had changed. He enjoyed school more, was more confident, and was learning with purpose. But what was really pleasing was that along with these positive changes he had not lost his capacity for fantasy. He still wrote imaginative stories.

Chapter Eight

Revelations of Understanding

I had planned the thinking books to encourage the students to think more about what they were learning and to link it with their experiences outside school. I had not thought that they would do anything more, so I was surprised when the children's entries gave me new insights into their learning and the effectiveness of my teaching. The books proved to be an extremely effective tool for probing their learning.

What the children wrote about the very first topic of the year, the initial white settlement of Australia, revealed to me that they were likely to construct different meanings from what I told them than what I had intended. Usually this happened because they did in fact relate the lesson to things they had learned elsewhere. Since it was the Bicentenary of European settlement the media had presented much information on the nation's history, but I assumed that the children would not have much of this knowledge because they had not been taught about it in school. I thought, though, that they would understand concepts such as convicts, Aborigines and the First Fleet. Indeed they did know something about these concepts, but as often as not that knowledge led them into misconceptions that hampered their learning.

One common misconception involved the role that Captain Cook played in the early settlement of Australia. The media had given space to Cook's voyage of discovery in 1770 as the precursor of the First Fleet under Captain Phillip that came in 1788 to settle, so that many of the children confused the two voyages. They formed the misconception that it was Cook who brought the First Fleet to Australia.

Jenny: 4 February

200 years ago capton Jams cook
descuved Australa on the first fleat.
this year we selabrate our bicentonary.
in that time we have manigid to bild
houses shops and schools some
abrignes are good people Australa
has a lot of native animels some
of them have strang names like
platpus wambat emu and kwala
and kangroos

Further confusion arose from the children's memories of our school production of the previous year: *Peter Pan*. Some mixed up Captain Cook with Captain Hook, as Ariana's (chapter 4) and Anna's (chapter 6) entries showed. I never found out whether this was connected with knowledge that Australia has crocodiles. Perhaps the confusion of Cook with Hook was aided by the message prominent in the media that the convicts and the Aborigines were treated badly, as one would expect from a villain like Captain Hook. That message may also have promoted the misconception that some children formed that the Aborigines *were* the convicts, brought to Australia in 1788.

Alice: 12 February

the abrijines was in jail the
abrynes was on the boat theirtr
visatt to go to go to Australia

The title 'Captain' itself caused confusion which I discovered through the thinking books. Anna (chapter 6) wrote, 'Who was the aborigines' captain?' Her experiences with captains had been restricted to sporting teams. She assumed that the aborigines must have been the convicts' opponents as they appeared to be the only other 'players' in the game.

Much of what the thinking books revealed to me was a surprise. I had not been aware that misconceptions on this scale could exist after my teaching. A further surprise was how often the children misunderstood the purpose of a lesson. Their entries showed frequently that they had learned something quite different from what I had intended. An example was a lesson on perimeter, where I thought I was teaching the children to solve a problem involving borders of a flower bed. I was very pleased with the lesson: the children worked well and enjoyed creating their own 'flower gardens', drawing a variety of flowers and measuring the borders. Their thinking books, however, showed that many had focussed on an irrelevant part of the lesson such as the type of flowers planted.

Lizzie: 9 March

At maths I Lent how to work out
metre sams and how some flowers
look like vilets.

Another instance of misunderstanding the purpose of a lesson occurred in a series of science activities on the topic 'air'. Different groups worked at different activities. After one session I asked each group to write what they had learned about air. The children in the kite-making group looked puzzled, and said 'Air? But we just made kites!' Although they enjoyed the activity and learned to make kites, they had not increased their knowledge about air.

Polly: 15 June

Today I leant in
sinec how to mak a kite and the
placers that you are not aposto fly
it arond and all ~~the~~ evencns
like the old aeraplans.

Allana: 15 June

~~TR.~~ Today in ~~Sices~~ Sience We learnt
about air we ~~lean~~ learnt how
to make kites fly. We also
learnt how ~~tr~~ to make a kite.
We also learnt ~~ho~~ ~~how~~ not
to fly kites near people
and not ~~f~~ to fly them near
~~Pow~~ Pawer lines and also

not to fly them near trees. It can be usefull ~~flat~~ fully if ~~ya~~ you are doing a projet ~~on~~ on air you will now alot about air.

The entries in the thinking books often led me to change my plans for the following sessions. The entries showed me whether the children had the understanding necessary to achieve the objectives I had in mind. Many times I saw that I must teach something else before I went ahead with my original plan, and in other instances I had to alter the follow-up session to introduce overlooked concepts or skills.

When I used the thinking books to make inferences about the children's learning I had to keep in mind that their understanding of the function of the books would affect what they chose to write. They might, for instance, write about an unusual aspect of a lesson because they found it more interesting than the main focus, or because it was easier to describe. I think this was the case with the lesson on perimeter using the flower garden. At least in these instances the apparent irrelevance of the entries alerted me to the need to investigate in other ways whether the children had grasped the point of the lesson.

In addition to providing me with insights into the children's understanding, the thinking books showed me the level of their interest and enjoyment in topics and activities.

Krysia: 31 May

Today I learnt about exchanging. When I was in grade preps my dad taught me these sums

but he did it the hard
way. I have a whole book of them!
at home. I didn't know how
to do them with the exchanging properly until this day. It was
fun doing maths today.

Vicky: 21 March

I Learnt in maths today
all about xof take away.
and plus. I love harde.
Somes its fun some
times I get my sumes
rong I like it wen I get
all of my somes write
I news the sumes for
maths and for qick suns.

Jenny: 26 February

Today at since I lirnt wich bottle
whod be easeyest to fill and
empty I got nearly all of the

wirkright it was very very very very fun weitested What vottles whad look like difrent ways up We lirnt about sinking and floting I like since it is fun.

There were negative examples also, for the children did not hesitate to use the thinking books to let me know when they had lost interest. Sometimes they did this subtly, as I think Catherine intended in the next entry.

Catherine: 17 February

Miss Suron I have rithen all I know about the tall ships and the ferst fleet you will hafto thech me more.

The thinking books not only told me how interested the children were, but also showed me what they felt about topics. This made me more sensitive than I might have been with topics for which the children displayed a wide variety of attitudes. Jenny and Lizzie, for instance, revealed different views of the Australian Aborigines, which I had to keep in mind while planning and running lessons.

Jenny: 3 March

why did the wite people spole the abrignies life? and why did the witemen take all of Australia? Mrs Swan I feel sorry for the abrigrines. Is ther sume way we can help?

Lizzie: 3 March

How come some Aborgons don't were cloes or sores How come some Aborgons reke cars for. Why do some Aborgins live in reked cars for.

Reading each separate comment day by day helped me understand how the children felt about each lesson, but I found that when I went back and read all the entries that a child had written I learned something different. For each child I found consistent patterns in the entries that told me much about their styles of learning and the strategies they employed. For instance, I found that several children regularly did not answer the question I had written, but rushed on to their next reflection. Others showed that they had fallen into a pattern where they used the same type of language and wrote the same style of question each day. I had not been aware of these consistencies until I read through the books several months into the year.

I had introduced the thinking books as a means of encouraging the children to be more purposeful and conscious learners, and had not thought that they would be so useful in revealing the children's misconceptions, misunderstanding of the purpose of lessons, learning styles, and interest in and attitudes towards topics. I meant the thinking books to help the children, as indeed they did, but in the things I have described in this chapter they helped me as a teacher, in guiding my planning of lessons and in making more meaningful my relationships with individual children.

Chapter Nine

Stephanie

Stephanie arrived new into the school from a nearby school at the beginning of the year. She was enrolled by her older sister. Her sister is fifteen years Stephanie's senior and requested that any correspondence or problems concerning Stephanie be directed to herself rather than the parents as their English is limited. Both parents were born in Italy, as was her sister, although Stephanie was born in Australia. She has no other siblings.

When I asked Stephanie about her home, I found that she had no responsibility for herself or her belongings. She was not expected to perform any jobs around the house. Her school bag was unpacked for her in the afternoon and packed again the next day. Her sister told her what to wear. All notices which were given to Stephanie to have signed by parents and be returned, such as religious education and swimming permission slips, were returned to school by her sister. A few days after I had given the class their first project to be completed at home, Stephanie's sister arrived at school to find out exactly what the project entailed, as she claimed that Stephanie seemed confused and anxious about it. When the projects were handed in, Stephanie's was of an extremely high standard with very detailed illustrations and written in handwriting which definitely did not belong to her. When I asked her to present her project to the class, she could not even read what was written.

All of the children in the class work daily on process writing. This entails work on individual pieces of writing for which they are responsible. My role during these sessions is that of a consultant, conferring with individuals or small groups of children about their writing. During the first couple of weeks of term, Stephanie would complain at the beginning of each session that she 'had nothing to write about'. She asked to work with a partner. I allowed this in the hope that it would motivate her or stimulate some ideas for her own writing. During the first four weeks of term she 'worked' with various partners but seemed to spend all her time talking about irrelevant topics. The only written work completed during this period was written solely by the other child.

Stephanie rarely made any contributions to class discussions early in the year. Occasionally she would raise her hand indicating that she had something to say and then ask a question quite irrelevant to the discussion. For example, during a discussion about the conditions on board the First Fleet ships for convicts, she put her hand up to ask if the class had sport that day as she had forgotten her runners. She tended to sit on the outside of the group of children and often played with another child's hair during such discussions.

At the beginning of the year Stephanie often seemed inattentive when I was giving instructions. She never attempted anything without first requesting help. She continually complained that she did not understand or could not complete an activity before attempting it.

Stephanie's early reflections in her thinking book regarding what she had learned revealed a lack of effort and responsibility toward her own learning. Her first three entries all commented that she had learned something but had forgotten what.

4 February

What did you learn about the early settlers? I fogot.

5 February

We saw a map and i lornt alot

What was it that you learnt Stefanie?

um i Don't know why but I

fogot

I interpreted these entries, and Stephanie's other early behaviour, as a plea to be left alone, that she had found that school demanded too much of her and the only way she could cope was by withdrawal. Her sister's well-meant management supported her in this action. If Stephanie persisted in it, then I could see that she would gain little from school, and would suffer years of mindless tedium before she could leave. I wanted to prevent such a waste.

A student's withdrawal is not easy to combat. Any threat, any criticism, would reinforce it, yet there has to be some coercion to break through the wall of passivity. The thinking books proved to be useful here. They were a compulsory task, so Stephanie could not dodge by not volunteering. They were individual, so she could not rely on another child to do it for her. They were written in class, so big sister could not help. They were used every day, so they could not be avoided by a small number of stock excuses that might help you escape from an activity that came round only once a month or so. There was no help for it, Stephanie had to write *something*.

I was careful with all the children to keep my entries in their books positive or at least neutral. This was particularly important with someone as school-shocked as Stephanie. When she found that she could not avoid the task of writing in the thinking book, and that I was not going to write that she was wrong or her spelling or handwriting were poor, she began to write a little more. It was, however, not related to the topic I had asked her to write about.

10 February

10.2.88
Yestorday I lornt at home how to do this thing that is Italian but I don't know how to say it in English.

In response to each of Stephanie's minimal and unrelated entries I wrote neutral directions, such as:

Yes, we learn at home and at school, ~~bt~~ but what did you learn during our maths activity today?

It took two weeks of this before Stephanie wrote an entry that related to the topic I had given her.

16 February

I have lorn abot the black people they were tiyed under the boat. They were alad on deck for exesidz.

Although this entry revealed that Stephanie confused the convicts with the Aborigines, I was delighted that at last she had shown some comprehension of the task. So I wrote in her book a positive response, only to find that Stephanie misinterpreted it. I had commended her for writing about the topic I had set, but Stephanie took it that I was pleased that she had written about the tying under the boat, so although the next day's topic was maths problem solving, she wrote almost the same thing again.

17 February

I did lornt abot the first fleet they were tyed under a boat the water was deep but I do not know how deep

I explained in my written response that I wanted Stephanie to write about the given topic of the day, and I was relieved to find that she grasped this. From then on her entries were relevant.

I imagine that it was partly because of practice and partly because of growing confidence that Stephanie began to put more detail into her entries.

1 March

A legen is Something abrigenn explan to tell you insten storys. I know two legens they are how the Brids got there coluer and How the kangroow got his tail.

I continued to support Stephanie with positive comments, but began to mix in suggestions that she write about how what she learned in school would be useful outside. She began to respond.

10 March

Today at maths we done some sums. I lornt that maths you do have to lorn just incase when you grow biger something hapens with the bank and you have to add up at home sumtimes i practes somes because i play scool I lorn alot by doing sums.

Stephanie's 10 March entry shows a great advance from the beginning of February. Not only has she written a lot more, and is relevant, she shows that she sees that school learning is useful. But even more encouraging for me was her note that she played school at home!

In my responses I encouraged Stephanie to continue to link school learning with life outside, and to ask questions on anything about which she felt unsure or wanted to know more. Her entries showed steady growth in active linking and in reflection on the use of knowledge.

24 March

Today in Maths we lornt how to tell the time and so did I. At fist I was worreyed because I thort that I wuld never know how to tell the time but now I do now how to tell the time. It is usful to na know how to tell the time because when you grow up if you have a meating for work you need to know how to tell the time. Or you can be late for scool if you dont know how to tell the time.

Stephanie's classroom behaviour began to change at about the same time that her thinking book reflections were changing. She began to attempt to complete her work before asking for assistance, and usually found that she could complete it without help.

Stephanie began to work on her own during process writing sessions after the fourth week of term. She began to produce some quite reasonable pieces of writing and no longer asked for topic ideas. Stephanie managed to organize conferences about her writing and before the end of term had made two of her stories into books.

Stephanie's participation in class discussions gradually increased during the later part of the term. She began to make some worthwhile contributions and ask some interesting questions such as: 'How did the white people learn to communicate with the Aborigines?'

The second project which was to be completed at home was handed in at the end of first term. Stephanie's was written in her own handwriting this time and she presented it to the class quite confidently.

She had not become totally independent, for the artwork was again of a high standard and obviously she had not done it. But Stephanie had come far since her withdrawn yet dependent days at the beginning of the term. I was not alone in recognizing this. Her sister came to tell me that Stephanie had said how much she had improved and how she was thinking so much better. I think it is unusual for an 8-year-old to recognize such a mental change in herself. At the end of the first term Stephanie asked to take her thinking book home to show her sister and parents how well she was doing and how she was a 'good thinker' now.

Of course the thinking book may not have been the sole cause of Stephanie's change in attitude and behaviour, but it certainly played an important part in raising her confidence and sense of control over her work. When I asked her at term's end whether writing in her thinking book had helped her with her learning, she gave a definite 'yes'. When I asked how it had helped her answer was far beyond what a withdrawn and negative little child could have said a dozen weeks earlier: 'Well it makes me think about what I use things for when I grow up and that. It's good for you to think about what you're learning and to ask questions. I think they're really fun too.'

Chapter Ten

Jenny's Book

Since I had bought the books and issued them to the children, they all looked the same on the outside. They had light blue covers, and inside were forty-eight pages of A4 size with faint lines fourteen millimetres apart. The extracts reproduced in this book are about half the actual size. The children wrote in pencil, sometimes coloured ones. As I wanted them to feel that they owned the books and what they wrote in them, I never tried to control their choice of colour, even when an occasional fad for pale yellow made it hard to read!

Of course some children wrote more than others, but most filled more than one of the forty-eight page volumes during the year.

The extracts from the children's books that I have used so far do not show how a book grew, or the pattern of my comments and questions, so this chapter presents a continuous section, the first twenty-two pages of Jenny's *Thinking Book*, covering the first two months of the school year.

200 years ago capton Jams cook
descuved Australa on the first fleat.
thisyear we selabrate our bicentennary.
in that time we have manigid to bild
houses shops and schools. same
abrignes are good people Australa
has alot of native anamels some
of them have strang names like
platpus wombat emy and kuala
and kangroos.

Good thinking Jenny.
Where do you think those strange names
come from? I am not shore
Can you guess? NO
They are aboriginal words.

On the 13 of may the first fleat started thare dangeres Jerney most of the passingers wher convicks some of the wherst times was running out of splise.

Why was the journey dangerous?

~~thare~~ becoas of the bad wether

food andwater sothe convicts wher given less and less food.

ther first stop was tenerife ther they got more foodand water then thay wher of a gen the next stop was Reo ther they got oringes fresh ~~veg~~ fruit wine and warter sper parts. at Reo the convicts when aloud to go on deck.

You have learnt a lot Jenny.

Do you eat any of those same foods?

Yes

The first fleet whent past van Demend's land to get to australia at first they cowld it new holend ther the prisers settled down.

Can you imagine what it must have been like for the convicts when they first arrived? it was terrebele be caus they set to work rite away and they wher very tieerd

They worked very hard, until the sun went down. What time do most workers finish work today? my dad cames home at six o'clock

In summer this is a long time before the sun goes down.

the first fleet hadavery long trip
Can you think of anything else that would take 8 months? sory but I ran out of time.

Today we thort about how it whold be to be a convict. And we thout how it felt to be gilty and we rote about it. the convicts must have felt terrible. ashamed and angry. sory lony. and very sad.
When have you ever felt like this?
neary all the day.

To day we arived at botny bay. rich or pore convickeds had to wirck. and if you did not wirck you got the lash of the whip it felt terubule. Miss swan prtenend to be our cmander (but she was not to bad, arfter all)

You have described here what you have done. I want you to write down what you have learnt.

Yesterday we lernt that it was very hard to cmenacate with the awrignys becaus they did not speak there langwige. it was very hard

When you were in Nepal, how did you communicate with people who didn't speak English?

I used my hands

Today at since I lirnt wich bottle whod be easeyest to fill and empty I got nearly all of the wirk right it was very very very very fun we tested What bottles whod look like difrent ways up. We lirnt about tinking and floting I like since it is fun.

Did you get your predictions correct?
How did you make your predictions?

today we made a concept Map I lirnt alot about the first fleet. Conecpt Maps are like the Meaning Of samthing and a bit like a jig saw pusel you write the thing

you Want to write aboute
and put it down like a map.
Good thinking Jenny
What did you learn by doing the
concept map? I Learnt What a
concept Map was. Can you see what use it would be? No
I don't think so
Today we Talked about
the abopigines and Mrs swan
red us a story. about the
aborigines lirnt same wase
to get waton and to cach
anmils for food
What questions do you have about our
work on aborigines?
why did the wite peoplE spole the
abrignios life? and why did the
witemen take all of Australia?
Mrs swan I feal sorry for

the abrigrines. Is ther sume way we can help? The aborigines want some of their land back. They are asking the Government to give it to them.

Today at since I lirnt haw to make plastersean flotl you had to make it into a boat it was very easy whanse I made a boat evry one whanted to copy me.

What made your boat a good design?

becas I made mine thin and the egers wher higher

today we lirnt nathing about abrigrines but I will tell you what I lirnt over the larst fue days. Over the larst fue days we talked about abrigines (not to much).

Mrs swan reid us a story

about abrignies I lirnt about
the life abrignys live and
some ways to get warter.

Why isn't water a problem for us today

becouse we have taps and over the years
we have invented lots of things

Good thinking Jenny. thankyou

today we did some more of our Project
today I lirnt some of the ways the abrignies
tort the children. How did they
teach their children? they told legends
from the dreamtime to explane thing.

Mrs Swan can I arsk you a qusine
what duse the story of tidlick the
explanl? It is supposed to explain
lakes and rivers I think. but there
wher allredy lakes and rivers thats whore
tidlick got all of the water from

today we did sume more of our
progects and I lirnt some
more storys from the dreamtime

I lirnt about the story of the wicked wizzed and about a trik (I have forgoten the trips name).
What stories do English people like to tell their children? My dad has reid me I am David and star fous red dirt

today we lirnt at since that the the nouth pole is only ice and tha soutth pole is land and we have to see mr bullick arfter school to get some ice

Today we did some of our projects about clothes that abrignes whor and why and we made a coat out of paper and we had to finsh the patton I lirnt that some abrignies whore difrent clothers to show What grop they wher in.

What people that we know ~~where~~ wear special clothes to show what group they're in?

gides scouts police men and ladys

That's right Jenny.

today at since I lirnt that we where to think like a sintenctest. (Sory I rote only a little)

How do scientists think?

they have to make a fere test.

Friday today we went on an icskurshen and I lirnt that abriginies are protesting to get there land back.

~~What~~ Why do you think they want their land back Jenny? becose the wite men are spoiling there land

Today at maths I learnt
how much egging a garden
needs by adding up the sides

Excellent Jenny!
Can you think of other situations
where you might work out a problem
in the same sort of way?

at Maths today I learnt
how to swap cards and
know how much we have
left by sums

That's good Jenny. What other
times would we use those sort
of sums to solve problems? gardang

today I was with Mrs Loukus
and we were testing foods
to see wich whood dezolve
and I lernt tha rice bubbles

coconut rice and cinamon
donot dezolve in cold water.

How might you be able to use this
knowledge in real life?

you might need to tell your mu
or when your in high school
you might need it for cooking

Good thinking Jenny.

today at sport I larnt a dance
and mrs swan tort it to us
befor. We lirn to dance becas
it is good excersize and
you might go to a disco
when your older,

That's good Jenny. I'm glad that you
are thinking about real life
situations that we can use the
things we have learnt.

Today we went to sport and I lirnt that you have to ceep in time tomake a dance lock good and I also lirnt that if you do exersize it helps asma.

That's good Jenny. You learnt quite a few things today.

today in hand writing we were learningto join our letters. We need to join our letters becas inthe fucher you mite be silly if you don't lern. Good Jenny. Can you think of why it is better to use joined writing? becaUse it look better.

Today arfter silent reeding we did story writing and I lirnt to write our owne books it is good. becas when you grow up you might be un ather and it is good to get prachdes

Very good thinking Jenny. What makes your ~~st~~ writing improve?

people giving me Idears and reeds other books. Excellent thinking Jenny.

today at since I lirnt that you can dessolve things in vinger. thing like shuger.

What might this be useful for Jenny?

Today at silent reeding
I lirnt that Mrs. Swan
gives us silent reading to
lirn to read proply and
inprove my reading.
Why is it important to learn
to read? becase athewize you
cauldnt read sines and books
and you wood be very bord.
today we read a story
could the easter rabbit
and I lirnt that the easter
bunny went in the night
and I lirnt that australa
has tacken some Idars
from the story. did you
know that there is much
more than an easter
bunny and fun. Jesus

died on easter day and
he rose agen it remineds
me of a bible virse for god
so loved the world that
he gave his one and only
son that who ever beleved
in him shall not die but
have etirnl life John 3:16

Very good thinking Jenny. You
know a lot of things about
Easter. It's really good if you can
remember and join up things you
know with things you are
learning.

Today at maths I lirnt how to
tell the time on a clock face
lirning to tell the time
is very usefull becas if you

don't lirn you wood be late for work and school.

That's good thinking Jenny. How are you going to make sure that you remember how to tell the time?

pracrdes on the clock.

Have you been doing this? Yes

Today at R.I I lirnt that Jesus is hear with us all the time. O.K

to day at maths I lirnt that you can use a plum line to see that things are strate. and I lirnt that virtical things go strate down. and horizontal things go strate across. and that you can

tell horizontal things
by looking at the
horizon becuse the
horizon is horizontal.

That's excellent thinking Jenny.

When might you use a plumb line?

When you whant to see if
things are strate. For example?

today we did some of our
projects and I lirndt that
canbra is a good place to go
and viset and I lirnt that
you can goi on a travel
around australea with out
leveing the room. That's excellent
Jenny - you need to use some
imagination though! What might you
see in Canberra?

Today at Librey I lirnt that facts means that some thing is true. Can you tell me a fact that you know? you are a techer. Good.
today we did some of our projeckts and I lirnt that port Jackson is the name of Sydneys port and I lirnt that if you tack a trip around australia you can lirn things on the way lick how meny contry thire are on the ege of astri and you can also have fun. Good Jenny. Have you ever planned a trip using a map? yes Mrs Swan
today we did languig and I lirnt that you have to know igzactly. what you are looking up befor you look it up in a dishanery and I lirnt that you can use

a dishnery to help you underst
things Good Jenny. What things does a
dictionary help you to understand? complac
ted things. Today at art I lirnt that
you lirn art becase some people
sell things that they make at
art and I lirnt that you can make
plays with things that you make
at art Very good thinking Jenny.

What useful skills do you learn at
Art? pottry puppets and payntings
to day at ponders I lirnt that
no bodys pirfict becase I hade
to get someone to ran forme
becase I hade a saw leg. and I lirnt
at swimming that it is hard to keep your self
amused when you have not got enything
todo. Can you think of other times

when you have needed to do this?

in the car on long trips and whating in long cues. How very true!

Today at maths I Learnt that if you do sums quick you can save alot of time and you get better evry day. quick sums are good for shops becase if you havn't got a cash register you will have to be very clever to wirk out the sums

That's right Jenny. I used to have a part-time job in a shop and I often needed to add things up in my mind very quickly so I got quite good at it.

From the outset Jenny was able to write a lot about what she had learned. She was far ahead of Stephanie, more focussed than Arthur, but less fluent than Krysia.

Jenny's first sentence illustrates the children's confusion of Cook's voyage of discovery with Phillip's of settlement. I think the abrupt start half-way down the second page is because I asked her orally what sort of supplies the voyagers lacked. I like Jenny's description on the sixth and seventh pages of concept maps, even though she dampened my enthusiasm for them a little by writing that she could not see what use they could be.

On re-reading Jenny's book, I notice that she often did not respond to my written questions. You can see that in her sixth page, where I asked about her predictions. Perhaps I should have checked on that, and insisted on response. But maybe that would have made the book a chore, a task to be done to satisfy me. Of course it *was* such a task, but I did not want the children to feel it was so. I wanted them to enjoy writing in their books, and to think they could write whatever they wanted, so long as it was about what they had learned, without correction or penalty of extra work.

On Jenny's ninth page she asks me a question. Although there are not many more examples in this section, in the rest of the book she often asked very good questions. One thing I do notice on reading her Book is how often she relates what she learns to life outside school; she usually can give a good use for her knowledge.

Jenny lent me her book so I could make a copy of it. I wish I had all of the children's books still, so I could look into them from time to time to see how they grew as learners during the year. They are, however, their books, and so at the end of the year they took them away.

Chapter Eleven

Myself as a Reflective Teacher

If anyone had asked me years ago whether I was a reflective teacher, I probably would have proudly shown them the separate column I had in my work program for reflections on the day's activities. Under that column they would have read 'Jade needs extra help with grasping fractions'. 'Didn't finish newspaper activity – need at least another hour.' 'Alison finished final draft of story – needs typing.' 'Con and Nick beginning to get a bit competitive esp. in maths.' At the end of each day I deliberately made time to think about the children and the day's work. I thought I was a reflective teacher. The introduction of thinking books in my classroom made me realize otherwise. Those so-called reflections I had been doing were really only surface thoughts. To become a truly reflective teacher, I needed to think far more deeply.

One of the key objectives for thinking books is to encourage children to question the purposes of classroom activities. Until they began to do this, I realized how seldom that I, myself, had really considered such fundamental ideas. Although I had thought about why I implemented various activities in my classroom, I had not thought deeply enough about them. I knew, for instance, that I taught the Law of Equal Additions so that the children could gain later a good understanding of subtraction, but I had not gone beyond that to think about the value of this work to the children's life outside school. The questions the children wrote about the purposes of activities went straight to the core. They forced me to justify each piece of content with reasons other than its use in preparing them for the next piece.

Tim: 11 April

Today in doble
rittin I didint now.
how to do dable riting
Why do we larnt how
to do doble ritting?

The children's questions forced me to recognize that I needed to address the issues personally first – not on a surface level but on a deep level. I had to consider why I chose certain things for them to learn and why I left out many others. I had to work out how these decisions fitted in with my philosophies about learning and teaching, what I really wanted the children to gain from their learning both immediately and in the longer term. I could not answer their questions until I had solved these problems.

My reflections affected my choice of classroom activities. Like most teachers, I have a few favourite 'fail safe' activities that I enjoy doing year after year. The justification for some of these activities became more difficult. I had to become honest with myself as I was forced to be honest with the children. Both my teaching and my learning became more purposeful.

The thinking books gave me a real opportunity to reflect on the various learning styles in the class. Reading through the individual thinking books gave me important insights into how the children approached learning tasks.

Jenny: 16 May

Today we where estimating things and I Lirent that if you try thing the first time you arnt very good at estimating but if you try to do things that you do all the time you get very good at things like estimating. I use estimating alot moastly time. I estimated when I cooked tea I had to estimat how long it whod take to cook the meal ~~and~~ that night we had tea at 7o'clock so I had to get tea redy by ~~[illegible]~~ 6othiry and I was right my estimat was right and it was a very good meal aswell.

Information about how the children learned helped me to organize lessons. Some children seemed to learn best by talking and asking questions initially, some preferred to listen and think, others needed to 'have a go' in order to stimulate their thinking. Jenny, in the previous comment, evidently showed a willingness to learn from her mistakes. Understanding this enabled me to allow for variations in the children's preferred learning styles when planning classroom activities.

Reflections on my experience as a teacher determined my personal philosophy of how children learn most effectively. This philosophy led to the thinking books, and in turn was affected by them. Indeed, I found that the thinking books forced me to become more reflective. They provided me with too great a wealth of information about the individual children, about what was happening in the classroom and about myself as a teacher, to ignore. I had not foreseen that all this reflection on learning would not only change me as a teacher but would also affect me as a learner. I began to think about my own style of learning, and how I might become a better learner. The thinking books changed my learning as well as the students'.

Learning to master a computer for use in the classroom was a good example of this. For years I avoided contact with the computer – almost priding myself on the fact that I had managed to get by quite well without it. I was unwilling to put myself in the uncomfortable situation of being a new learner. I had attended numerous in-service sessions and workshops using computers as part of our school professional development program. I managed during these sessions to complete the tasks while learning nothing. I had made up my mind that I did not need to learn this.

Through observing some of the interesting uses of computers in other classrooms I eventually admitted that it was a permanent feature of our education system, and that I was denying both myself and the children in my class access to a potentially useful resource.

I enlisted the help of an enthusiastic colleague who attempted to teach me about computers and how I might use them in class. I never felt very confident – she rushed me on to the next step before I had grasped the previous one. I became frustrated as I had not yet learnt anything I considered useful. I was ready to give up. I then realized that I was not practising personally what I was trying to encourage children in my classroom to do. I was taking no control over my own learning. I was passive, not questioning someone else's agenda. I decided to take control, and worked out exactly what I wanted to find out and why. I established how I wanted to use computers in the classroom and what I would need to learn in order to do that. I thought about the most appropriate means for finding this out. By taking the initiative, having a clear purpose in mind, I was able to control and use the many learning resources available to me. Through my success in mastering the use of the computer, I had learnt something far more useful: how to master my own learning.

The experience of encouraging children to become reflective learners resulted in not only the development of myself as a reflective teacher but also as a reflective and more effective learner. I had not expected that when I began the thinking books. I had intended to change the children, and indeed I did. But the thinking books turned out to be more powerful than I knew. They changed me.

Chapter Twelve

Five Years Later

The children are 13 now, and at secondary school in year 8. Much has happened around them, and they have done lots of things and had other teachers, so the *Thinking Books* cannot be given all the credit or blame for how they have developed. Nevertheless, I wanted to find out how things are with the children, to see whether they remember the books and whether they think about their learning. Especially I wanted to check on Stephanie, Arthur, Krysia, Ariana and Anna.

I could not find Ariana. Her family had moved from the district, and the school had no record of where they had gone. But I did talk with the other four, and with Catherine, Paul, Kevin, Tim and Jenny.

Krysia

Krysia has had a lot of success at school. At the end of grade 6 she won a scholarship to a private school, and in her first year there won the academic award. Her school reports show As in every subject, and her teachers commend her for her achievement and attitude. Her favourite subjects are art, English, history and home economics. She enjoys oral work, especially, as she says she loves to talk. Everything is going well for Krysia. Her artwork is published in the school magazine, and last year and this year she won certificates of excellence in the talent quest run by the Science Teachers' Association. Krysia says she has many friends, and is active in music, art and sport. Naturally, she is enthusiastic about school.

When I asked about her learning, Krysia said she does think

about it and about how she learns best. She makes sure she has absorbed knowledge by putting it into practice straight away. She does, however, forget things once the need to recall them in a test has passed. She asks lots of questions in class, even though she is aware that some of her teachers do not appreciate it:

> It doesn't worry me because my friends all like me asking questions. Most of them are too shy to ask, but I know that if I don't understand some of them won't either.

Krysia remembers the *Thinking Books* clearly. She has kept hers, and sometimes gets it out to read.

> I remember thinking for ages about what to write. I found it a hard thing to do. I remember you making us think about purposes for what we were learning. I still do that now at times but I try to focus on just what I need to know for exams or what I need to learn to move onto the next thing. Sometimes it's hard to see a purpose until much later when you learn the next step and then it becomes clear. Other times it's easy like home economics because it's a real life skill. Often I don't make connections until much later, like I didn't see the point of learning about a circle's circumference until we started learning about area.

I am glad that Krysia is happy and getting on so well at school, but cannot claim that my teaching or the *Thinking Book* had much to do with her success. Almost certainly she would have prospered anyway. Her first entry in her *Thinking Book* showed that even then she reflected on what she learned ('I rekon it was very crule') and was ready to ask questions. The *Thinking Book* merely gave her scope to exercise these attributes.

Catherine

In grade 3 Catherine was far behind Krysia in language skills and maths concepts, though, as she showed in her criticism of

do think, though, that it was the year when he began to grow up.

Anna

I found less change in Anna than I had in Arthur. In grade 3 she had been quiet and unreflective, wanting approval and so needing reassurance and certainty about what was required and what was correct. She is still quiet, and finds it difficult to talk about herself, but had interesting things to say about her learning.

Anna said she learns most successfully when working in a group. She listens to other people's ideas before she makes her mind up on what she thinks herself. She works well with others, and likes to talk things through to help her understand. She said that her teachers encourage their pupils to think about their learning and to ask questions, which she does do.

Anna rates herself as just average academically, although her school reports show all As and Bs. She dislikes mathematics because she cannot see its purpose, but enjoys commerce because, she says, it is a practical, real life subject. Anna hopes to go on to university after school, and would like to study something like business management.

Like Krysia, Anna kept her *Thinking Book*. She remembers well writing in it each day, and says she enjoyed using it.

> You could see your own development – you know, what you learnt. It made you really think about what you were learning.

Paul

Paul is quiet, willing to answer questions but not comfortable talking about himself.

Like Arthur, Paul does not remember much about the *Thinking Books*. He does recall that I encouraged him to write questions, which he thinks was useful for him because he does not like asking questions publicly.

Paul hopes to find a career in computing, though strangely he does not enjoy mathematics because he cannot see its application.

He says he tries to see connections, and likes it when he suddenly sees the point of something he learned earlier.

Kevin

In contrast to Arthur and Paul, Kevin remembers clearly writing in his *Thinking Book* about what he learned and the purpose of learning.

> I still use that skill, especially in English where our teacher encourages us to do that.

He says he looks for links.

> At the moment we're studying animals in geography. It's good because I've done a fair bit about animals before and I've read a lot of books on animals. I can use all that knowledge.

Kevin says he thinks about what he is learning, and asks questions if he does not understand,

> but not too many because teachers get sick of too many questions.

Kevin enjoys all aspects of school. His favourite subjects are sport, science and Japanese. His reports show almost all As. He won an academic achievement award last year, and expects another this year. Also he has won several sports awards. Kevin plans to go to university, although he has so many interests he does not know yet what he might study.

Jenny

Jenny, like Kevin, enjoys school. She has almost straight As in every subject, won an award for academic achievement last year, and won the school prize for community spirit and leadership. Her favourite subjects are English and singing. She would like a career in music or in counselling children with problems.

Also like Kevin, Jenny remembers her *Thinking Book* well.

She kept hers, and reads it at times. She recalls being anxious about it at first, because she did not know what to do.

> After I had read what you'd written, though, I realized it was O.K. You were just interested in what we thought – we couldn't go wrong.

I'm glad that Jenny remembers that the *Thinking Books* were never corrected or criticized. Jenny went on to say,

> *Thinking Books* are good for a person like me because I tend to accept things and not question them. *Thinking Books* forced me to question what I was learning. I still tend to accept things too much. I always think the teacher must be right. I should question more.

Although Jenny says she thinks the teacher must be right, the fact that she thought of that indicates that she does realize that teachers can be wrong. Whether it was the *Thinking Books* or something else that was responsible, she is much more thoughtful about learning than I think most 13-year-olds are.

Tim

The *Thinking Books* might have worked for Jenny, but I do not think they did much for Tim. When I asked him what he liked about school, he said 'Recess, lunch-time and three o'clock'. He prefers the hands-on activities of physical education, cooking, metalwork and woodwork to academic subjects. He is making reasonable progress in his learning, with 'B's in most subjects, but his reports show that his behaviour causes him problems.

> Oh, you know, that's just me. I get bored with things. I like to *do* things.

Tim recalls clearly the purpose of the *Thinking Books*.

> We used to write about what we learned and why it was useful. It was good because it made you think about things.

Although Tim recalls the strategies and sees their use, he says he rarely puts them into practice now. He sometimes sees the point or the relationships between things, but does not think much about learning.

> I just do what I have to do. Teachers concentrate on my behaviour, they are not very interested in how I learn.

Tim wants to be a motor mechanic. Maybe he would think about his learning if he was taught things he wants to know.

Stephanie

Although I was pretty confident that Stephanie would continue to improve, I was not certain. Would she have regressed to the dependent, totally passive, isolated child who, at the beginning of grade 3 was going through school, and even life, without reacting or learning anything? Or would she be getting by, but not really making much progress?

I found a girl full of life, bubbling with enthusiasm for school. Stephanie had no trouble with the transition from primary to secondary school. She enjoys having a variety of subjects, and said her favourites are English, science and geography – English because she thinks she has particular skill in creative writing, and science and geography because she likes finding out about things to satisfy her curiosity about the world. She has lots of friends at school, and feels comfortable and happy there.

Stephanie said she does think about her learning. When she begins a new topic she finds it helpful to draw up a question sheet with everything she wants to find out about it. Then she can check whether she has learned all she wanted to. Another deliberate technique she uses is to divide a topic into manageable sections, which she says allows her to learn more thoroughly than others. She uses a tape recorder, as she likes to verbalize her thoughts about what she is learning. Stephanie thinks she takes a little longer than other students to learn, because she studies topics more deeply and likes to know all the little details.

Stephanie had clear memories of grade 3 and her experiences with *Thinking Books*. She recalled the initial difficulties she had with the task, but said that she always enjoyed reading what I had written in response to her. She remembered how excited she was when she began to improve, and taking her book home to show her sister.

When I asked Stephanie if she saw the purpose of the *Thinking Books*, she said:

> Yes it helped in lots of ways. We had to really think about what we'd learnt through the day. You encouraged us to express ourselves better. You made us think about why we were learning certain things.
>
> Year 3 was a big year for me. In prep and years 1 and 2 I really just came to school and did what I was told. In grade 3 I really started to think – I was actually thinking about what I was learning and why. I wrote more and found I wasn't scared to write. The more I thought and wrote the more confidence I got. It gave me confidence to ask questions about things. Actually I have a real reputation for asking questions now. I always ask questions in school because I want things explained properly. I often ask what the purpose of learning things is – especially in History (I think to myself – Oh, that's in the past, let's learn something more interesting, but I guess it's good to build up your general knowledge).

I suppose the *Thinking Books* touched all the children to some degree. Some, such as Krysia, may not have needed them. But with others, especially Stephanie, I believe the *Thinking Books* changed their lives.

Index

Alice, 25
  extract
    12 February, 72
Allana
  extracts
    9 March, 46
    12 April, 8
    15 June, 73–74
Anna, 49–58, 71, 117
  ability, 49–50, 57, 121
  ambition, 121
  effect of thinking book on, 57–58
  extracts
    4 February, 51
    18 February, 51
    29 February, 52
    25 March, 56
    28 March, 53
    30 March, 53
    19 April, 54
    11 May, 56
    8 June, 55
    9 June, 57
  family, 49
  linking of knowledge by, 55–56
  neatness of, 49–50
  personality, 49–50, 52, 121
  questions from, 51–54, 121
  recollection of thinking book, 121
Ariana, vii, 29–36, 71, 117
  ability, 29
  extracts
    4 February, 30
    10 February, 30
    23 February, 30
    29 February, 31
    4 March, 31
    8 March, 32
    17 March, 32
    21 March, 32
    12 April, 33
    15 April, 33
    2 May, 34
    16 May, 35
    17 May, 35
  linking of knowledge, 33–36
  parents, 29
  questions from, 33, 35
  reaction to thinking book, 35
  understanding of purpose, 30–31, 36
  watershed in interest, 34
Arthur, vii, 59–69, 111, 117, 120, 121, 122
  ability, 59, 119
  ambition, 120
  art and, 59–60
  creativity of, 62, 119

extracts
10 February, 60
16 February, 61
9 March, 61
30 March, 62
21 April, 61
6 May, 62–63
11 May, 63–64
18 May, 65
20 May, 67
26 May, 67–68
7 June, 65–66
family, 59, 66
independence of, 59, 61
invention of headings by, 66–68, 119
learning style, 65, 68
perception of purpose, 60–61, 63–65, 69, 120
personality, 59, 119
recollection of thinking book, 120
reflection by, 65–66
stories by, 59–60, 69
taste for fantasy of, 60, 61–62, 65, 69
thinking book and, 60–61, 66–68

Carle, Eric, 24
Catherine, 117, 118–119
ambition, 119
extracts
17 February, 76
10 March, 46
24 March, 1–2
13 April, 42
language skills, 2, 118
later progress, 119
learning style, 119
recollection of thinking book, 119
children's origins, 2
confidence, 20
construction of meaning, 70

Dibley, Linda, 4
discussion, 8, 10

Hynes, Damien, 3–4

Jenny, 88–111, 115, 117, 122
ambition, 122
extracts
4 February, 71
26 February, 75–76
3 March, 41
22 April, 45
16 May, 114
27 May, 47
later achievement, 122
linking of knowledge by, 111
recollection of thinking book, 123
responses to questions, 111
Justin
extract
11 May, 12

Kevin, 117, 122
ambition, 122
enjoyment of school, 122
extracts
4 February, 40–41
26 February, 9
27 May, 48
linking of knowledge, 122
recollection of thinking book, 122
Krysia, 15–23, 24–25, 68, 111, 117, 118
ability, 15, 23
English skills of, 15
extracts
4 February, 17
5 February, 7
11 February, 18
25 February, 14
4 March, 18–19
22 March, 19–20

13 April, 20–21
20 April, 21–22
17 May, 22
31 May, 74–75
later success, 117–118
learning style, 16, 20, 118
linking of knowledge by, 15–16, 18–21, 23
mother, 15
participation in discussions, 15, 16, 20
perception of purpose of learning, 21, 118
precision of, 15
questioning by, 15, 16, 18, 118
recollection of thinking book, 118
use of other knowledge by, 16, 22–23

language skills, 11, 12
learning
children's perception of, 25–28
cooperation in, 24–28
distinction from doing, 8–10, 14, 30–32
passive, 3, 37, 116
styles, 26, 45, 51–52
lessons, purpose of, 3, 6, 25, 43–45, 57–58, 72–73, 112–113
linking of knowledge, 6, 16, 27, 68, 70, 84
Lizzie
extracts
3 March, 77
9 March, 72

meaning, construction of, 4–6
Michelle
extract
30 March, 12
misconceptions, 4, 70–72

Nicole
extracts
undated, 26, 27

Paul, 117, 121–122
ambition, 121
extract
20 June, 44
recollection of thinking book, 121
Polly
extracts
16 March, 9
13 April, 13
15 June, 73

questions
children's, vii, 5–6, 7, 37–48, 51
about purpose of lessons, 44–45
about topics not understood, 42–43
decline in, 37
factors discouraging, 38
role in learning, 39
types of, 39–41
teacher's, 13, 19
responses to, 111

reflection, vii, 8, 10–13, 41

social skills, 24–25
spelling, 15, 23, 48, 57
correction of, 2
Stephanie, vii, 79–87, 111, 117, 125
enjoyment of school, 84, 124
extracts
4 February, 80
5 February, 81
10 February, 82
16 February, 82
17 February, 83
1 March, 83

10 March, 84
24 March, 85
13 May, 43
27 May, 48
independence of, 79–80, 86
family, 79
linking of knowledge, 84–85
reaction to thinking book, 86–87
recollection of thinking books, 124–125
relevance of thinking book entries, 80–85
sister, 79, 81, 86, 125
thoughts about learning, 124
withdrawal and participation by, 79–81, 86, 124–125
Swan, Susan
as learner, 4, 115–116
as reflective teacher, 112–116
children's personal interactions with, 39, 52–54
effect of thinking books on, 112–116
encouragement by, 20–22, 33, 37, 41, 51, 82–84, 121
feelings of, 11, 13

Tasker, Ross, 3
thinking books
appearance of, 88
as probes of understanding, 70–74
criticism in, 7, 22, 81
effect on lesson planning, 11, 74, 76, 115
effect on teacher, 112–116
feedback in, 8, 13, 38–39
frustrations with, 7–8
headings in, 66–68
introduction of, 6–7
ownership of, 88, 111
purpose of, 14, 38, 70, 78, 112
children's perceptions of, 17, 23, 46, 50, 74, 123–125
questions in, 7, 19, 38–46
reactions to, 7–8, 10, 35, 123
recollections of, 118–125
revelation of interest by, 74–78
revelation of learning style by, 77–78, 113
skills in, 8
training in, 10–11
Tim, 24–25, 26, 117, 123–124
ambition, 124
extracts
8 February, 39
11 April, 113
indifference to learning, 123–124
reaction to school, 123
trust, 20

understanding, 4–6, 25

Vicky, 26
extract
21 March, 75